HAY HOUSE BASICS

MEDIUMSHIP

WITHDRAWN

MEDIUMSHIP

An Introductory Guide to Developing Spiritual Awareness and Intuition

GORDON SMITH

HAY HOUSE

Carlsbad, California • New York City • London
Sydney • Johannesburg • Vancouver • New Delhi

First published and distributed in the United Kingdom by:
Hay House UK Ltd, Astley House, 33 Notting Hill Gate, London W11 3JQ
Tel: +44 (0)20 3675 2450; Fax: +44 (0)20 3675 2451; www.hayhouse.co.uk

Published and distributed in the United States of America by:
Hay House Inc., PO Box 5100, Carlsbad, CA 92018-5100
Tel: (1) 760 431 7695 or (800) 654 5126; Fax: (1) 760 431 6948 or (800) 650 5115
www.hayhouse.com

Published and distributed in Australia by:
Hay House Australia Ltd, 18/36 Ralph St, Alexandria NSW 2015
Tel: (61) 2 9669 4299; Fax: (61) 2 9669 4144; www.hayhouse.com.au

Published and distributed in the Republic of South Africa by:
Hay House SA (Pty) Ltd, PO Box 990, Witkoppen 2068
info@hayhouse.co.za; www.hayhouse.co.za

Published and distributed in India by:
Hay House Publishers India, Muskaan Complex, Plot No.3, B-2,
Vasant Kunj, New Delhi 110 070
Tel: (91) 11 4176 1620; Fax: (91) 11 4176 1630; www.hayhouse.co.in

Distributed in Canada by:
Raincoast Books, 2440 Viking Way, Richmond, B.C. V6V 1N2
Tel: (1) 604 448 7100; Fax: (1) 604 270 7161; www.raincoast.com

Text © Gordon Smith, 2017

The information given in this book should not be treated as
a substitute for professional medical advice; always consult a
medical practitioner. Any use of information in this book is at the
reader's discretion and risk. Neither the author nor the publisher
can be held responsible for any loss, claim or damage arising out
of the use, or misuse, of the suggestions made, the failure to take
medical advice or for any material on third party websites.

A catalogue record for this book is available from the British Library.

ISBN: 978-1-78180-817-7

133·91

Printed and bound in Great Britain by TJ International, Padstow, Cornwall.

This book is dedicated to all the great mediums and psychics of the past.

To those I knew personally:
Mrs Jean Primrose, Mr Albert Best and Mrs Mary Duffy, to name but a few.

To those who follow, I say, always carry the torch with pride and sincerity.

Contents

List of exercises

Introduction

Mediumship is something that has been a part of my life as far back as I can remember. As a small child I suppose I could say that I was very sensitive, to the point that I would feel other people's heavy emotions or pain; I could be lifted by their joy and happiness in just the same way. It's easy for me now to recognize that I was a natural intuitive who was very often affected by the atmosphere around me.

The function of a medium is to be the conduit between this life and the afterlife or spirit world. Every medium is intuitive or psychic, but not every psychic is a medium. With the luxury of hindsight, I can clearly see that my sensitive nature as a child was part of what was to build to become the gift of mediumship, which I first experienced at the age of six, going on seven.

Even now I can say it is one of my most vivid memories from early childhood. I was playing on my own in the small garden at the front of my house when I saw a man coming towards me from the other end of the street. He looked familiar and I soon recognized him as a friend of my parents who had the very unusual nickname of Ummy. He was a frequent visitor to our home and every time he came he would bring presents or give us children a couple of pennies each, usually after he had won cash at the horse races. The racetrack was a big part of his life.

I remember feeling happy to see him and I wanted to run towards him, but my feet seemed to be rooted to the grassy ground beneath me. I also recall feeling that I was in a bubble or membrane of sorts, which felt safe and had a dreamy quality. It also had a sort of buzzing sensation that was pleasant.

Ummy smiled at me the way he always did and his eyes looked so alive and happy. He was singing softly, to a tune I'd never heard, 'We will be buried in Dalbeth.' I had no idea what this meant, but it was infectious, so I began to sing along.

I've no idea how long he was in front of me, but as he began to move steadily away in the direction he'd come from, I felt that the bubble I was in had burst and instinctively I ran into the house.

My mother was standing at the kitchen sink peeling potatoes.

'Mammy, Ummy was here, Ummy was here!' I blurted out in pure excitement.

My mother's reaction was to drop what she was holding. Her eyes widened with fear as I sang the little song: 'We will be buried in Dalbeth.'

The next thing I knew, I was being smacked and shouted at and I had no idea why my happy news had made my mother so scared or angry.

It wasn't until many years later that my mother told me she'd been so stunned by what I was telling her that she'd completely freaked. Ummy had died in an accident, but my parents hadn't felt that they needed to explain this to their younger children. Also, they had been left to pay for his burial and they had very little money, so they had him laid to rest in what was known as a pauper's grave in a remote part of a cemetery outside Glasgow called Dalbeth. Both my mother and father were proud people and hadn't spoken to anyone about it because they were ashamed that they couldn't afford a proper funeral for their friend.

People have often asked me if I was ever frightened as a child when I encountered spirits from the other side, but I honestly didn't ever feel fear of any kind. The reaction of the people around me gave me much more cause for concern than any spirit being.

Even though I came into this life with natural psychic abilities, I still had to learn how to hone and perfect my gift. I had to know how it all worked and why I had it, and also what purpose it could serve.

Now, looking at the combination of sensitivity and mediumship has allowed me to understand more about the mechanics of my gift and to simplify it and break it down, so I can explain it much more clearly to those who wish to learn how to develop their own abilities.

Most mediums I've encountered on my travels have at some point on their journey met a teacher, someone who could help them to come to terms with their spiritual gifts and direct them in how best to use them. I was very lucky in that I met my teacher when I was in my early twenties, a time when my mediumistic and psychic abilities had been reawakened after the death of a friend, who had appeared to me looking as real as Ummy had in my childhood experience. It was because of this incident that I found Mrs Jean Primrose, a great lady of spirit who would become my mentor and teach me the simple values and moral codes I would need in order to use my gift for the benefit of people all around the world.

The great thing about Mrs Primrose was that she provided a foundation for her students to grow from. Her teachings were simple and clear, and everyone who sat in her class was made to work on themselves first before extending their thoughts to the spirit world. She wanted us all to know that much of what happened in our mind came from *us*, and that with the correct mental exercises we would be able to know the difference between our own thoughts and imaginings and the impressions put into our mind by the spirits around us.

It takes quite a time to develop enough to use your gifts of psychic awareness or mediumship and that is because you need to learn to be responsible for everything you say to people who come asking for your help. I remember thinking that because I had had psychic experiences in my early life, I would be able to learn all this stuff very quickly, especially now that I had a teacher like Mrs Primrose. How wrong I was.

Mrs Primrose started by teaching me to still my mind during meditation sessions. She would allow new students like myself to meditate for a while, and when she brought me out of the quiet state, she would ask me to describe what had been going on in my mind. I would always do this in great detail and be surprised when she dismissed my ramblings with a nod. I naturally assumed they were brilliant. Inevitably I was left wondering about what went on in my mind during my meditation sessions.

One night after our session Mrs Primrose took me aside and asked me if I would sit with my eyes open during the next session. She wanted me just to observe the other students and try not to think about them or what was going on with them.

I always did what Mrs Primrose asked of me and so the following week I did just sit quietly and observe the other students. After a while, as I looked at them, I began to wonder what was going on in this person's mind or that person's, but then I remembered that my purpose was to observe rather than assess or judge. I found this quite difficult at first, but then I began to be still and not follow my own thinking. I believe this was the first time that I separated my awareness from my actual thoughts.

I soon realized that my thoughts only passed through my awareness like leaves floating on top of a stream and if I chose not to pay attention to them, they would float on by. It dawned on me that this was something I'd have to bring into my meditation when I was sitting with my eyes closed.

I'd no sooner had this realization than my teacher looked in my direction and nodded. It was the end of the session and people were being brought out of the meditation. I couldn't wait to talk to Mrs Primrose and tell her of this great Eureka moment.

I must have been sitting in that class for more than a year by then, and all that time my teacher had been listening to the nonsense that I'd been coming out with at the end of my meditation and never actually commenting on it. Now I understood that she'd been monitoring my progress all along and instinctively working out just where I was in my development.

How exciting it was back then to be guided by a very experienced person through the corridors of my mind and learn about the psyche and the world of spirit. It was amazing, especially as until then I hadn't been able to talk to people about my gift or my thoughts on life after death. I'd always assumed that people would laugh at me or think I was some kind of freak. It had never occurred to me that what some saw as freak, others saw as unique...

I am so grateful to Mrs Primrose for teaching me to stay grounded in my work and my understanding of spiritual practices. Without her down-to-earth teachings and guidance, I wouldn't have been able to advance to where I am today. The foundation she gave me has allowed me to travel around the world lecturing and demonstrating my gift to thousands of people, as well as to explore further and come to some amazing new realizations about mediumship and the spirit world. It also gave me the confidence to allow psychical researchers at Glasgow University to test my abilities and publish scientific papers based on their findings.

I find that today I tend to work more with the teaching of mediumship because so many people are waking up to the fact that they are having mediumistic or intuitive experiences and are seeking explanations for them, along with the opportunity to develop their abilities to the highest level possible. Everyone who has spiritual gifts deserves the opportunity to be gently directed through the maze that is the human mind by the steady hand of an experienced teacher. Also, having a plan for the development of your gift makes the road ahead so much clearer and a lot less congested.

Some years ago I was asked to take my teaching out to Germany, where many students wanted to put together a course for developing mediumship that would be easily understood and serve as a template for others to follow in the years to come. I thought this was a wonderful idea, so I put together the course of spiritual development that I am now sharing with you in this book.

I would like to use this opportunity to clear up some of the misconceptions about mediumship and simplify the process of developing it, but more than this, I truly want you to know that it is more than okay to explore your spiritual gifts and share them with those who have need of them. After all, something is only really a gift when you can share it with others.

I'd also like you to know that as a medium you should be responsible for what you give to others. I see so many people who call themselves mediums and psychics who upset people with their work. There are even those who frighten people with off-the-cuff comments about their future or personal details.

It's a huge responsibility to work with the public, especially when you're seen as someone who might bring hope or healing to another person. You should therefore have a clear understanding of the process of mediumship before you start to use it on the public. This means you have to be clear and balanced both mentally and emotionally. It is for this reason that we will start by looking at the highs and lows of the mind.

Chapter 1

THE HIGHS AND LOWS OF THE MIND

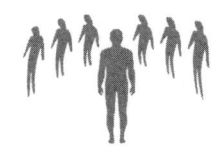

Before beginning any mediumship training, it is my way to give an outline of the mind and how it can be prepared for working with the spirit world. I always share this information at the start of a new course and I'm sharing it with you now so that you can understand your own mind and how it can be affected by both the spirit world and your own emotions.

Starting out...

To start your spiritual development, I would always recommend finding a good teacher or spiritual group where you feel accepted and find it easy to trust those around you. There's something about working as a group that I've always found helpful for my spiritual work. I know many mediums who don't 'sit in a circle', as it is known, and some who never have, and often they'll protest that you don't need to develop your spiritual gifts 'in circle' and if the gift is natural, it will proceed on its own.

To some extent I'd have to agree that a natural medium would probably find a way to use their special abilities in their life, but I must say that it was my circle that really shaped me as a person and taught me to have great respect for the spirit world and the way that those who are there very lovingly guide us whenever we need them. One of the things I tell all my new students is that spiritual development is about making a better person for spirit to channel through, and that is what happened to me and has happened to so many I know who started with a group. There are many Spiritualist churches and other organizations that offer people the chance to develop in a circle and you should be able to find one in your area.

That isn't to say that you can't develop on your own. If you are going to do this, though, make it a special practice, just as you would if you were going to a development class. However you choose to start, try to be as committed as you can to your development. (*For more on both circles and sitting alone, see Chapter 6.*)

Whether you are on your own or in a group, the process is in fact the same: you begin your spiritual development by sitting quietly and trying to enter a meditative state. It is wise to sit where you feel comfortable and balanced. If you are in a room in your own home, then make sure it is a room you feel good in. Always try to start at the same time and to prepare the room first. Some people like to light a candle or burn incense, but whatever you do, it's about turning your mind in a more spiritual direction before you begin your practice – and that means clearing the mind.

Clearing the mind

I look back now at what Mrs Primrose taught me about listening and observing without thought or judgement and understand its true value. The problem that most students have when they start out is they believe that they are getting more messages from the spirit world than they really are. They assume that when they sit and close their eyes every thought or conversation that passes through their mind is coming from a source other than their own thinking mind.

Like my teacher before me, I listen to each student and try to hear in the tone of their voice where they are truly speaking from. I've learned how important it is to take note of everything they tell me, even if I know that what they're saying is nothing to do with the spirit world or has no bearing on their spiritual development. A good teacher should always observe and listen to their students.

Most people at this early stage are getting a tiny percentage of spirit messages through their mind and a large percentage of their own thoughts and imaginings, based on their emotional state before they began their practice. If you've come into your meditation with a mind full of things that are happening in your everyday life and you can't switch from this kind of thinking, chances are your session will be focused on those situations and you'll have no chance of getting any proper meditation done, let alone receiving any messages from the other side.

That's why it is very wise in the early days to allow the day you've just come from to wind down in your mind before engaging in any meditation practice. It's also good to talk to other people for a while, just to let go of anything that might be sitting at the front of your upper thinking mind. This is the part of your mind that you use in your normal waking day. Arriving a bit early to meditation class, even if only by 10 or 20 minutes, will give you time to let off steam, maybe share some of what has occurred in your day and relax into the idea of moving from an everyday situation into a meditation practice. You really don't want to take your day into the quiet space of your meditative mind if you can help it.

One of the best things I remember doing before my own development class was deliberately walking to it after work, rather than getting on a bus. There was something about that early evening walk from the north to the west of Glasgow that cleared my mind and allowed me to release many of the confused thoughts that had gathered during my working day. I honestly think that the time I spent walking was my first real experience of mindfulness: I was just walking and observing without assessment or judgement. By the time I reached the church, my mind was almost empty.

It's also good to take on board the notion that your development class is on a different level from the everyday stuff. The very idea that you're going to a special place might take your mind to a higher vibration before you sit in your session. When you can do this, you're getting into the right state of mind to begin your development.

Any form of spiritual connection is about raising your awareness to a higher state. Remember that spirits exist in that higher state, as they are part of the divine.

Overcoming fear

So many students come to me and tell me that they get amazing messages from the spirit world but they're scared of the spirits who bring the messages. Or that they'd love to sit in a development group, but they're afraid that they might go into 'some sort of funny trance state' and never come out of it. Or that they're never sure of the spirits – some might be bad, etc.

It is because of ideas like this that I've devised a way of helping people to get over their fear of spirits and spiritual development and showing them that there's nothing to fear but fear itself.

Take a look at the diagram below. The great thing about it is that it's easy to see how the human mind works when affected by its own emotional states, both high and low, positive and negative.

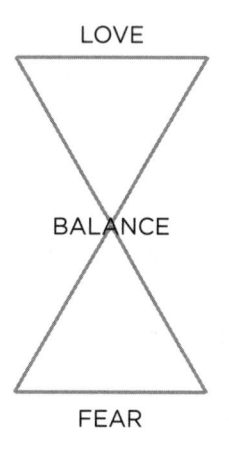

LOVE

BALANCE

FEAR

A representation of the human mind

In the diagram you can see two triangles, one on top of the other. The lower triangle represents the lower, more human part of the mind, and you'll notice that the word 'fear' is written across the base of it. This is there to remind you that our very lowest mental states, where we encounter depression, anger and jealousy, are born out of fear. It is also in this very heavy, dense part of our consciousness that we experience the most human desires, things like lust and greed and of course *ego*. It's this part of the human mind that we want to move away from on our spiritual journey.

The word 'balance' runs through the part where the points of the two triangles touch, and this is where we want to have our awareness during our meditations. When we can reach this area, we're getting into the proper frame of mind to open up to a higher source. That source is the spirit world, our spirit guides and teachers who watch over us and who can communicate with us and give us guidance once we have a clear, balanced mind for them to work with.

It's so important to learn that negativity is a human thing and nothing to do with the spirit world. The sooner you learn this, the sooner you can make progress in your development.

Imagine for a moment a person who has a belief in the spirit world but whose awareness is constantly dragged down to the lower realms of thinking. The spirit world they experience in meditation might appear quite dark. Such people often refer to 'bad' or 'dark' spirits and 'places where the spirit can get stuck' and so on. But these descriptions come from their own fear, not from the spirit world.

I honestly feel that if your mind is full of fear and dread then you aren't in the right place to develop mediumship.

Remember, a medium is someone who helps people who are afraid, not someone who projects their own negative imaginings onto others.

It's quite easy to see this happening in the behaviour of a new student and it's certainly easy to hear it in the things they describe. For me, a person like this is immersed in the lower part of their mind, the bottom triangle, where fear is controlling their thoughts.

Whenever I encounter someone who has psychic episodes and experiences but whose mind is filled with fear, I suggest that they start their development by attending relaxation groups and very gentle meditation classes where they aren't expected to do any mediumship or psychic exercises, just relax the body and quieten the mind. Once they are able to lift their mind up, away from their own fearful thinking, then they are better prepared to make progress in self-awareness and meditation under the guidance of a good teacher.

One of the German students in a group I took several years ago would break down and cry during her meditations and shake with fear as if something terrible had happened to her, when in reality she'd only sat down with a small group of other students, closed her eyes and tried to quieten her thinking mind and sit in her own inner space. But her own inner space was filled with fear and dread.

This was something she'd been experiencing for many years and it kept her awake for long periods of time at night when she should have been sleeping.

She explained to me that she had a fear of letting go and that the idea of not being in control of her thoughts was very frightening to her. I found this fascinating, because she really was only being asked to sit quietly and learn how to meditate. It's very interesting how some people see meditation as something mystical rather than relaxing or contemplative.

But I had to deal with my student, and I did, as it was important that she conquered this fear, otherwise she would never move on in her development, not to mention her life.

Instead of sitting her in the meditation group, I gave her guided meditations where I would suggest images, places and situations of a relaxing nature and talk her through each procedure step by step. She was easy to relax and she stayed focused, it seemed, on every suggestion I made. The only time I witnessed her brow furl with confusion or her body twitch was when I paused for a moment so she might process my words.

It became clear to me that this very nice woman didn't want to be with her own thoughts unless they were controlled and guided. She really wasn't happy in her own space or her own mind. I wondered what could possibly have caused this in an adult.

I spent some time talking to her and trying to encourage her to talk to me, explaining that if she could find the source of this fear, we could fix it, but she wasn't ready. It was six months before I finally got her to open up. Then she spoke of how as a child she'd been told that if she was bad or didn't go to sleep when asked, ghosts and demons would come and get her in the night.

How ridiculous! What were those people thinking? If you want a child to sleep, why on earth would you put fear into their small vulnerable mind before putting them to bed?

It's also incredible how many people suffer from similar fearful thinking. This woman herself had other fears, which she realized came from a similar time in her young life. Again we were able to talk about them and I was able to help her to rationalize her thoughts and move into a more balanced place in her mind.

When she realized that she was in control of her thinking and not the other way round, it gave her the strength to change her thinking habits and build a stronger mind-set, which she then took into her meditation. Within the space of a year she was meditating without fears and tears, and more than this, she was truly learning to open up to her gift of mediumship and healing, which she now practises very successfully seven years on.

So many people come to my groups with similar hang-ups and setbacks and without the understanding that most fears like this can't actually harm us, they're just something we've been told. It is the teller's *intention* that leaves the lasting scar on the young mind.

Here's an exercise that I used successfully with this woman. You might like to try it too. Dealing with our fears and imbalanced emotions is the first real issue we face when we undertake any kind of spiritual development.

Exercise: Balancing the mind

❖ Sit on a straight-backed chair with your back straight and your feet flat on the floor.

❖ Relax each time you take a deep in-breath and release any tension with every out-breath.

❖ Visualize my diagram of the two triangles (*see page 8*).

❖ Try to be aware of your thoughts as if viewing them from a distance. Are they in the lower triangle of the diagram, i.e. heavy and negative, or in the upper triangle, i.e. positive and joyful?

- If your mind is heavy and your awareness is sinking down to sad or negative memories, just breathe and remind yourself you are seeking balance.

- You will instinctively know when you're in balance, as none of your thoughts will affect your state of contentment, and all your thoughts will pass through your mind without having any effect on it.

- Once you're in balance, slow your breathing and slow your need to think up or down. Just hold the balance of your now quiet mind without any need to follow your thoughts.

Know your own mind

One of the questions I'm most frequently asked by new students is: 'How will I know what is truly coming from the spirit world and what is coming from my own mind?' The best way to know this is to know your own mind. This is so important for anyone who embarks on a spiritual path.

Take a look back at the diagram of the mind (*see page 8*). All of us can move up and down through the different levels. Our life circumstances can propel us up to the very high end, where we find love, joy and laughter, and just as easily drop us down into the pits of pain and despair. When you are serious about developing your mediumship, you need to be able to put yourself in the middle of those two triangles and work from a point of perfect balance, even when everything in your own world is pulling you up and down. I always try to hold on to a message I once received from my spirit guide: 'When all around you is in motion, be still, and in your stillness, control all that is around you.'

Start by asking yourself about your usual level of thinking. Are you a person who thinks negatively about yourself, your prospects or your life in general? Are you a person who is always full of hope and whose thinking lifts you up when you've been put down? Are you someone who can always take an optimistic view of life, past, present and future? Are you someone who finds a way to rationalize all of life's ups and downs and who doesn't often react emotionally to situations? Are you balanced?

Like most people, I always assumed I was a very balanced person, but when I began my development I found that I had a habit of being self-deprecating. I could applaud everyone else's efforts, but never my own, for some reason. I also had a terrible habit of looking at things in my own life with doubt and fear. I found it hard to be positive about my future and spent far too much time worrying about death and dying when it came to my nearest and dearest.

Learning about my thinking mind gave me a much deeper insight into myself and my emotions. So I recommend taking the time to work on yourself in this manner and dedicating the early sessions of your meditation practice to observing what happens in your inner space when you sit quietly.

What happens to your thinking in these sessions? Do you immediately think of getting a message for someone else? If so, ask yourself why this is the first thing you want to do. Do you think that you'll never reach a high level of meditation? If so, look at why you are set on defeating your purpose.

Questioning your thinking will enable you to grow appropriately and in a steady, balanced way. It will allow you to question things that are happening in your inner world and why they are happening. Thoughts don't just happen on their own. What's behind them – fears, judgements, emotions?

Examining your own mind shows that you want to develop mediumship for the right reasons and in a balanced way. If you can sit in your practice each time and simply get to know your own mind, rather than be in a hurry for instant success, then you're in the right place to move on.

It is this balanced, contented state of mind that you need to reach each time you sit in meditation. It isn't something to experience once, but every time. It's part of your meditative practice to bring your mind into balance and hold it there, no matter what emotions or feelings pass through your being. Just be still and *hold that balance*, even if your imagination starts to light up with pictures or colours, or you hear internal conversations. Don't get carried away and follow any of the impressions, thoughts or feelings that may come to you. You need to become an observer – a cameraman rather than the subject of the film. The whole idea of this process is to have control over your awareness and not be pulled up or down by your emotional thinking. Remember, your awareness is the stream, not the leaf that floats on top of it!

From this point of balance, you will have an overview of your thoughts, feelings and desires and can become truly discerning about the true you, the spiritual you that is about to flourish. Not only can you look down on the old you, but you can look up and see what lies above you. You can learn how to go up and let the higher energies influence your mind.

Letting love in

The upper part of our mind is where we experience the highs of life, such as joy, happiness, compassion and of course *love*. As nice as it would be, none of us can live here throughout our life, but as a spiritual student it is your aim to lift your thinking to a point where you can at least see the positive rather than the negative. You have to find ways to let love into your life!

I know that when I first began to sit in development I felt all the worries of my own world nagging at me, and fear was never too far away from my thoughts. After all, I was very young and had a wife and two young sons to look after, and any parent knows the weight of responsibility that can bear down on the mind at such times.

I wanted to grow spiritually and I knew in my heart that I was a medium, but the world I lived in was heavy and often short on positive goals to aim for. Nonetheless, I followed the drive that was in me and made myself face my fears and fight the urges that said life was too tough. Luckily I always had a kind of mental reflex that naturally found positive answers to problems.

One instance that comes to mind was when I was working as a hairdresser in a salon where every client had more need to discard emotional baggage than hair. One day I was faced with a woman in her late thirties who had lost her husband and her family home and was now living with her two teenage sons in cramped conditions in a friend's house. She was having a terrible time of it and had come into the salon to have a dry haircut, the cheapest thing on our price list. I think she just needed to be with people who wouldn't add to her troubles for a while.

It just so happened that there were no other clients in at that time and she told her story to me and the rest of the staff. She wasn't asking for answers as much as unburdening herself, I suppose. It was hard to listen to a woman whose future was so bleak and who seemed to have no resolve or energy to go on, but something stirred in me and I knew that there were solutions to her problems. This stirring wasn't coming from my psychic gift but my attitude, which I now realized had begun to change since I'd been sitting in my development class.

As I remember, I told the woman that she was looking at her whole life as one big episode and if she did that, she'd always be facing a mighty wall of hopelessness. I recall advising her to look at the first thing she needed and to make this her goal. Once she'd accomplished this, even if it was only a small success, she could celebrate it and progress from there. Her problems seemed too huge for her to even think about tackling, so it felt right to advise her to turn them into progressive steps to build up minor achievements until a sense of accomplishment replaced the feeling of hopelessness.

After that, she would pop into the salon for a cup of tea and a chat from time to time and inform us how she was getting on, and in a series of events over a six-month period her life began to move upwards. She first got herself and her boys a decent house from the authorities and shortly afterwards came a part-time job, followed by a reason to live.

I'm happy to say that this lady became my friend and still is today. She has a degree from the Open University and her work now is counselling women who are going through what she once did.

For me, this is what natural mediums do: they take darkness and turn it into light. Everyone knows life has ups and downs – a life has to contain both – but to develop spiritually you must find a way to move through your life and take some measure of control when you can. That is part of being a medium. So, when everything seems to be moving in a downward spiral, look up. Through this one action, directions can be changed.

Just as the word 'balance' runs between the tips of the two triangles and indicates to us where our awareness needs to be when we're working with the spirit world, so the word 'love' runs across the top triangle and indicates what we're working with. This triangle has its point facing downwards and the sides extending outwards, showing the expansion of the upper part of the mind. If you can learn to lift up your thinking, you're preparing your mind to love and to feel love.

More often than not, a medium works in the energy of a person who is very down, sad or broken by life's tragedies. Doing this work takes a lot of mental strength and a very positive attitude – a medium should always be able to look upwards when the recipient of their gift doesn't know how to.

Teaching your mind to sit at a higher frequency also means you can truly begin to feel love for yourself. It is so important to know love in yourself before you share it with others, because the real work of a medium is about sharing love and reconnecting the ties of love that have been severed by physical death.

I don't expect you to get a strong connection with spirit in the early part of your development process, but I do expect you to try. By this I mean you should dedicate yourself to a meditation group or practice and learn how to put the world aside and devote this sacred space and time to making your mind stronger, clearer and more balanced. With each attempt to do this, you will allow the spirit guides around you to build a connection with you at a higher level - a love level.

Once you've found that you can sit with a balanced mind, above your old fears and habitual thinking, you're ready to proceed a little further down the road of spiritual development.

Chapter 2

SITTING IN
THE POWER

It's easy to think that meditating is simply a case of sitting down, closing your eyes and telling yourself to relax. This is fine for the beginner who needs to get to know their mind, but as you progress you have to improve your awareness of body, mind and spirit. You have to sit in your own silent mind. This simple practice could be one of the most important things you do to improve your mediumship.

Stilling the mind

I've mentioned how in the very early days of my development I found it hard to switch off my thinking when I was asked to meditate. If anything, I found that when the intention was to be still, I had the impulse to think *more*. This is what happens to most people when they start to meditate at a deeper level. Either that or they fall asleep, because their mind is too tired to undertake mental exercise for any length of time.

Most people also find that their body becomes uncomfortable when they are asked to sit in the same position for half an hour or more. This is because they are being asked to be more aware of themselves than they are in their everyday state of mind where their awareness is filled with so many distractions.

While going about our daily life, it's normal for us to be thinking of so many things that we forget to pay attention to our body. We never think of how to walk, talk or even breathe – it's all automatic. But during the early part of our development, we need to become as aware of our body and thinking mind as possible. We need to get used to the sensation of our body relaxing and going into a peaceful state without overthinking about what will occur next.

The idea is that the body can become separate from the mind, and the mind can observe and control the body and take it into an in-between state somewhere between wakefulness and sleep. To get into this slightly altered state of mind is the goal – nothing else at this time.

It took me a long time and many attempts to understand this process and reach a state of mind where I became aware of a silence in myself that brought about a feeling of patience, relaxation and stillness – a state where I could observe without reacting.

Try it with this very simple exercise. It is real training for the mind – training that prepares it for what is to come.

Exercise: Being content in your own quiet mind

Study this exercise and then take yourself through each step. In your early attempts, give yourself 10 to 15 minutes for it. You may wish to use a timer until your mind begins to tune in to the time passing while you meditate.

It always makes good sense to sit in a quiet place where you know you'll be undisturbed. Try to use the same room or place of meditation if you can; having the same familiar atmosphere each time helps you to relax.

❖ Sit comfortably on a straight-backed chair with your back straight and your feet flat on the floor.

❖ Close your eyes and start to breathe slowly and deliberately. Be aware of your chest rising as you draw air into your body and falling as you release air.

❖ Relax your shoulders and feel the rest of your body relax into the chair.

❖ Stay focused on your breathing, but don't try so hard now – let your body find its own natural rhythm. Just be aware of your breath.

❖ If thoughts begin to appear in your mind, let them pass through. Don't attach your awareness to them, just breathe and let them go.

❖ Be aware of the atmosphere around you and notice how still and quiet it is.

❖ Sit for a while in the quiet atmosphere and slowly breathe it into your body until you find your mind reflecting the stillness of the empty space around you.

❖ Notice how balanced your mind has become, with no need to move up or down and no need to think or accomplish anything. You are in your own space and completely clear of emotion, empty of thought.

❖ Sit in this balanced, clear state and allow your mind and body to appreciate it.

❖ Now breathe deeply and deliberately to fill your lungs with air again.

❖ As you do this, start to become aware of your body resting in the chair.

❖ With every new breath, become more alert and aware until you feel that you are completely awake again.

Remember, all you have to do to come out of any meditative state is to breathe deeply and deliberately. Never think for a minute that you aren't in control of going into or coming out of meditation. Your breath is your doorway.

This meditation can be performed any time, as it is only about you and its value is for you alone. But I would recommend that you carry it out just once a week for 10 to 15 minutes to start with and then build up to no more than half an hour. When you can do this comfortably, try to sit for 40 minutes without either falling asleep or coming out of it with more questions than answers; both of these scenarios should tell you that you aren't achieving the stillness of mind required.

This exercise is essential at the beginning of spiritual development, but maybe you noticed there wasn't anything about contacting spirits or getting messages or clairvoyant images of any description?

As I mentioned earlier, it's necessary for all mediums to be able to separate their own thinking mind from the messages that come from the spirit world. If you get to know how you think, you'll find it much easier to distinguish your thinking from any outside source that can influence you.

I also believe that it's very good practice for any student of mediumship to have a meditative exercise that they can use to keep their thinking mind clear and uncluttered whenever they need to. I know that this exercise has helped me to become more grounded when things in my life have got turbulent. Just sitting in my own space and becoming balanced, body and soul, has been a proper reality check.

Now would be a good time to make some notes on the thoughts, feelings and any other sensations you experienced during your practice. If you are sitting with other people, it can be valuable to share these after the session, because when you express what you've just experienced in words, it can bring more understanding to your mind.

If you choose to sit on your own, keeping a diary of what happened will provide the same benefits. When we write down our experiences, they can become more solid and evidential; also, some of them might have more relevance when reviewed at a later date.

I've sat with people who've had a mind full of information 'from the spirit world' but no clear idea of what any of it meant. What it really meant was that they had no control over their thinking and saw their mind as a busy mail system where any being could leave a message. It also meant that they assumed that the spirit world was less than perfect, as it had given them garbled messages.

The idea here isn't to get to know more about the spirit world in any case, but to get to know more about *yourself*. This simple practice gives you the opportunity to build your mind into a strong, healthy faculty that you can trust. It isn't good to say that you get all sorts of messages coming through your mind and that you've no control over it – that's simply being weak-minded and gullible. I don't allow such behaviour on my courses; my students are always taught to find out *why* something is happening when they're uncertain.

The spirits we aim to work with are intelligent beyond measure and you would do well to remember this rather than assume they'd fill a person's head with rubbish. That always makes me think of people who play with ouija boards and how either all the spirits they contact are dyslexic or they're just making it up.

Rather than try to get all sorts of messages, at this stage you should simply try to reach a quiet state of mind. And you should take this practice seriously. It's difficult for most people to still the mind quickly. Our whole life is based on patterns and logic, and when we're asked to meditate, such things are left to one side.

I remember that in my early training I would sense and feel so many things when I was asked to use this practice. I know it took me at least 18 months before I managed to care less about what my thoughts were trying to do and start to master the art of not trying.

Understanding your own power

It is at this point that you might start to perceive other sensations when you meditate or sit in a spiritual circle. For example, I would become aware that my heart seemed to be palpitating or that there was a vibration surrounding my entire body. At times my logical mind suggested that the chair I was sitting on was moving.

So many of my students over the years have asked me about such sensations. I find that most understand immediately when I explain to them that it certainly isn't the chair that's moving, and it isn't their physical body either, but their light body or aura that's vibrating.

Understanding the aura and how it works will make the whole process of mediumship much clearer for you. There's more on this in the next chapter, but for now let me tell you that for me, the penny dropped when I was undergoing some scientific tests at Glasgow University conducted by Professor Archie Roy and his associate, Trisha Robertson. During one particular test I was wired to a heart monitor as well as other machines that recorded bodily functions. The basis of the experiment was to see what happened to a medium's body when they went into meditation or an altered state of consciousness.

Now when we meditate, our bodily functions should slow down, especially the heart rate and the breathing, and to all intents and purposes that's what all the machines were telling the investigators, but I felt that my heart was racing and my entire body was vibrating with energy. When the findings were revealed to me, I honestly wondered for a moment if the machines were working properly, because the rate of vibration around me was quite strong, yet no one mentioned it, and although I felt that my heart rate had accelerated, I was told that it had slowed by more than half the normal rate.

I was pretty shocked by this, but suddenly the penny dropped: if I wasn't the one moving and the chair I was sitting on was static, then there had to be another force around me that was pulsing.

I'd only been developing for a few years at that time, but it became clear to me that the feeling of movement around and through my body was probably what was called the aura or, as I now refer to it, the light body. This is our own subtle energy in a lighter form; it's much lighter than physical energy and that's why it's almost undetectable by the human senses.

As you continue your practice, the intensity of your meditation will build and at some point you'll be able to sense your own light body or auric field pulsing or expanding around you. It's the first step to what some mediums refer to as 'sitting in the power'. This refers to the fact that when you work as a medium, it is the power of the spirit around you that is fuelling the demonstration or reading.

Let's look at this subtle energy in more detail.

Chapter 3

WORKING IN
THE AURA

Sensing your light body and learning how it is involved in your spiritual work can help you to understand so much about mediumship and even spiritual healing. I've come to learn that I can only feel the vibration of spirit close to me through my auric awareness. My physical body isn't as sensitive, so doesn't recognize it, but my light body does.

The light body

It is the light body that we often see in depictions of saints and angelic beings in religious art. More often than not, we see the main spiritual figure with light surrounding their head in the form of a halo or emanating from their body into the atmosphere around them. I've always found it interesting that artists assumed that elevated spiritual figures were bathed in light that glowed and expanded to encompass all who looked upon them.

Psychics and mediums often describe seeing the auric field of a person as a light emanating about five to seven centimetres (two to three inches) from their body. There are people who can even see colours in the light body and can gain much information from this.

As a small boy I often saw light around people, and even animals, when they were near to me. I assumed that everyone saw this light and it was only as I got older that I learned that most people close to me had no idea what I was talking about. If I asked, 'Can you see the light around that woman?' all I'd get was funny looks.

In my early experiences involving spirit I would actually feel this light. During these episodes I always experienced a sense of heightened vibration around me. It was difficult to explain this to people. It's only now, after many years of working with spirit, that I know that this sense of accelerated pulse when I'm tuned in spiritually is because my own vibration has to accelerate to meet that of the spirit world in order for there to be a connection between the two worlds.

I think back to the buzzing or pulsing sensation that held me in a sort of bubble when Ummy appeared to me that day in broad daylight. The same was true of any other real spiritual connection I made as a boy. Even now, as a man, when I encounter spirit at a deep level, the same vibration occurs, and I still see light around most living things.

I remember in my late twenties having my eyes tested, as this heightened sense of sight was beginning to intensify and I would see light emanating from the bodies of people like the shards of light that radiate out of the sun. At the time I had 20:20 vision and no defect in either eye. So that was another time when I got funny looks when I described the things that I could see.

Many people do see the aura, though, and not only mediums. I've met people on my travels who don't know anything about mediumship but who see faint glowing waves of light around some people's head or shoulders. Many of the healers I've worked with not only see the aura of their patients, but sense it too. Some have a similar experience to my sense of buzzing and others talk about sensing a bubble of sorts around a patient's physical body but not on it.

The go-between

The aura is actually the go-between, the point where the spirit world can interact with human consciousness. People who've had no experience of spiritual development but have had what they would term 'psychic' or 'empathic' experiences quite often refer to a strange sensation that they find hard to put into words. This is because they aren't familiar with the idea of a body of light around them, a sort of extrasensory part of their being.

Most people try to explain such experiences according to their physical reactions, yet the very nature of this type of phenomenon would suggest that it isn't physical at all.

'Something or someone touched my shoulder – an invisible hand,' I recall a woman telling me after she had walked into a so-called haunted house in Scotland.

I told her that a spirit couldn't physically touch her, but if her sensitivity was expanded because she was on high alert, then her light body, which vibrated at a rate closer to the spirit world, might sense a touch that felt physical, though it actually wasn't.

The light body can bring information to you through feelings and sensations rather than through the usual five physical senses. It gives a sense of knowing at the very centre of your being. It is the subtle part of your consciousness, the early warning system that alerts you when something is wrong, even though nothing appears to be out of the ordinary. When you walk into a friend's home and know that there has just been an argument, even though the people there are smiling at you as though all is well, it's your aura that is picking up the energy and emotions that are held in the atmosphere.

This more sensitive part of you is what is active if you are a medium or sensitive, psychic or intuitive. Sensitive people are those who are born awake, as it were. I'm deliberately using the word 'sensitive' here because the function of a person with this faculty is to sense things that others quite simply can't.

As a small boy I'd often sense things that my siblings and parents could not. On one occasion I became aware of a situation that was worrying my parents and, without knowing how, saw the outcome and reported it to my mother and father.

It happened on a Sunday afternoon. I was playing with toy cars behind the sofa in our living room when I overheard my parents having a very worried-sounding conversation about my older sister Joan, who was around the age of 18 at the time. She'd told them that a young man she'd met was taking her for a short drive, and she was excited because he had a new car, which was quite a big thing back then. Only about an hour or so after she'd left, my mother started to become anxious and nag my father, badgering him with questions like 'Where the hell is she?' or 'How long will she be?' Obviously he couldn't give her the answers.

I remember feeling very unsettled as I continued playing behind the sofa. Then I became aware that there was something shaking or vibrating around me. My body felt stuck for a moment, then I had a real feeling of being with Joan and the young man. The moment passed and I reacted quite spontaneously, standing up and speaking directly to both of my parents, telling them, 'Joan is in a police station in Carlisle. She's fine and you'll hear about it soon. She'll be home tomorrow.'

Carlisle was about 95 miles away, over the border between Scotland and England.

Imagine how parents would react after a sudden outburst like this from their young son. Shock, I think, would be the first reaction, and so it was in this case. Then my mother shouted at me to get out of the house and play like a normal child.

The following day nothing much was said about it, but everything I'd told them turned out to be true. So I got some more funny looks from my parents and my big sister. I also recall that there was a look of great relief on the face of both my mother and my father. Oh, and just a little bewilderment too.

As I look at this situation now, with much more understanding of what happened, I can see that as a natural sensitive I'd become connected, through my auric awareness, to my mother's anxiety and somehow tuned in to my sister, so I was able to give an answer to my mother's questions in the way that a seer or psychic might have been able to. This wasn't mediumship, as those answers didn't come from the spirit world or a spirit being, but the subtle force that links to the spirit world can access information in this world too, a bit like the phenomenon known as remote viewing, in which things can be seen that are way beyond human sight. This is why I want to highlight this incident, as it shows that mediumship and events of a psychic nature have a common link, and that is the aura or light body.

Understanding natural sensitivity

As a child I honestly had no knowledge of the workings of things like the aura, or even the spirit world, but throughout my life I've had many experiences that have shaped my understanding and I do believe the reason for this is so that I can explain it to others on the path. If I'd had someone to clear my spiritual path like this when I was young, it might have made a great difference to my emotional intelligence and given me a better grasp of what was happening to me. On the other hand, all things have their purpose and without my own struggles perhaps I wouldn't be writing this book right now and trying to clear up some of the misconceptions that surround the world of mediumship.

I talked earlier about the first experience I had regarding Ummy, when I felt as though I was held in the moment and there was a kind of buzz around me. Now, looking back at this, I can see that the feeling around me was my own auric field being activated in order for the spirit of Ummy to communicate with me.

In actual fact, that same sensation was there in all of the spiritual phenomena that I experienced as a child or young man. It was this that made me look more closely at the energy around me during my own development. I wanted to know what was happening to my body and my mind whilst I was meditating or working as a medium. This was one of the reasons why I wanted to take part in scientific experiments at Glasgow University. I've always wanted to find out more about what makes a person a medium, or more sensitive than others.

Remember, I use the word 'medium' to describe a person who brings messages from the other side, from people's loved ones who have passed on. I use the term 'psychic' to indicate someone who can gain knowledge about a living person's past, present or future, as I did in the case of my sister. Both medium and psychic are likely to be sensitive to atmosphere and other people's emotions, but the psychic will work from empathy: they feel what others are experiencing, physically or emotionally. Some can pick up sensations from a room or place. If their aura can link with the aura of a place, they can give exact descriptions of the historical events that happened there. People who do this kind of thing can sometimes appear dramatic or even hysterical when they describe their feelings and findings, and they should note that they're only *reading* a message – there's no need to *be* it.

There's much more to learn about all of these things. When you can see that there's more to you than just a body made up of matter that works with five physical senses, then you're ready to work on expanding your mind to get to know your inner and extended self and, eventually, spirit.

Understanding your senses

Have you ever had similar experiences to the ones I've mentioned? Have you sensed something that has occurred miles away from you? Have you had an encounter with the spirit of a loved one who has given you information that you couldn't possibly have gained using your five human senses?

If you have, try to see these experiences as I have: as not happening *in* you, but *around* you and *because of* you. Although sensitives often feel that their experiences are happening in their physical body, on closer examination they find that they first happen around them and they pick up on them because they are sensitive.

Are you always having these experiences? Are you always in a heightened state? By this I mean do you feel that you'd like to tone down your light body because it's always activated, always on? If this is the case, then please carry on with your development, because all natural sensitives should learn how to switch their awareness on and off.

This is as simple as turning your attention away from any spiritual thoughts when you ground yourself in reality. When you open your eyes at the end of the meditation, for example, take a moment to be mindful of where you are sitting. Stretch your body, breathe and just try to be present in the here and now. (Some people teach complicated systems of switching on and off, but it really is just as simple as you make it.)

I am reminded of a man I will call Rob for the sake of this story. He called himself a medium and a big part of his life was going around Spiritualist churches in Scotland and giving people messages from their loved ones in the spirit world. On occasion, as a sensitive, he would give readings about a person's life.

Now if Rob had been the invited medium then this would have been fine, but he was never to my knowledge invited to work as a medium or in any other capacity by any church or group I know of.

Nevertheless, at the end of the session of mediumship Rob would tell people that while the real medium had been giving messages to the congregation, he'd also been tuned in and he too had a message for them. He described himself as always being open and said that his light was so bright that spirits always came to him, even when a genuine medium was working in front of him.

The sad fact was that none of Rob's messages ever made any sense to anyone. In some cases he actually offended or upset people and more often than not he'd be asked to leave the building to prevent this happening.

At the end of one of my own sessions I recall him asking me if I could see his light. I thought for a minute before answering him and then asked him to tell me about it instead. He said that he didn't know how to switch it off and that was why he was getting all the messages for people.

I asked him why the messages he was getting didn't mean anything to the people he shared them with and he said it was because his light was so bright that it was attracting too much attention from the spirit world. So it was the spirits who were confused and nothing to do with his ability to give messages at all.

Rather than go on with our conversation, I invited him to come and sit in my circle, where he could learn how to switch his light off and, with the proper time and training, learn how to really switch it on.

He refused my offer and I was sorry because I honestly wanted to help this sad man become grounded. It was my deepest wish to get him to see that no one could be that open all the time, and that as nothing he said made any sense to anyone, he wasn't a medium, or even psychic at all.

It was clear to me that it was his wish to be a medium but, like so many people I've met over the years, he wasn't willing to put in the time, effort and true devotion it takes to do the work properly.

Understanding the auric connection

This is a good point to look at your own psychic or sensitive episodes and see if you can understand the auric connection in what has happened to you.

It's so clear to me now when I look at the events that occurred in my late teens and early twenties, just before I went into my spiritual development class. I once walked into a nightclub when I was 19 years old and as I stepped over the threshold I felt a horrible sensation vibrate through my entire body. I had no idea what it was, but I turned about and went home. The following morning I read in the newspaper that a man my own age had been killed in a stabbing incident in that very club. Did I sense that? I can't say for sure, but something around my body told me not to enter. Was this my sensitivity?

I would say that it is always a good idea to make notes of such episodes and try to see where they fit into your development. For instance, in my case the Ummy experience was most definitely a spirit message, of that I have no doubt. I saw a vision of a man I didn't know had died and he gave me information that I couldn't have known. The Joan experience was a psychic one: I tuned in to the living and came up with an answer. The nightclub experience felt very sensitive and psychic, but it wasn't mediumship – I had no sense of any spirit warning me, this was coming from my gut – so I'd say it was more down to being sensitive to time and place than anything else.

I really urge you to monitor and record any experiences you have in your dreams or your meditation, and especially in your everyday life. Try to get to know your own brand of sensitivity and what it's trying to tell you about the nature of your gift or gifts.

I haven't always followed every instinctive feeling, by the way. You, too, may have sensed that something was going to happen and, instead of acting on it, gone against your senses and suffered the outcome. I remember many such times, because until you can truly trust your inner self, your intuition, your natural early warning system, you'll end up walking into situations you know you shouldn't.

Once, for example, I drove my car to a friend's home, and as I parked at the side of the house I had a sense of foreboding and just knew that my car was going to be stolen. Imagine how stupid I feel now as I write this, but it was one of those moments of doubt when I went against my gut, even though it had always stood me in good stead. I think we have to do this sometimes in order to truly appreciate our natural sensitivity.

For almost an hour I sat exchanging small talk with my friend until finally he asked me, 'Are you concerned about something? Only you seem a bit on edge.'

At first I tried to make an excuse, but then I confessed that I was worried about my car. I can still see his expression as he tried to understand why. He told me that it would be fine, as he didn't know of any incidents of car theft or vandalism since he'd lived there, but to reassure me he suggested I move it so that we could at least see it from his window.

It was one of those moments when you don't understand what has just happened. As we both stood and looked at the empty space where my car had been, I again noticed his expression, and this time it was he who appeared anxious.

'It should have been fine,' he said to me in a very apologetic voice.

We both knew that there was nothing either of us could do other than alert the police to what had just happened.

*I recall that after we'd done all the official things
with the police reports and so on, my friend did ask
me if I also knew who'd taken it and where it was
now...*

Exploring auric energy

We all have the ability to develop our sensitivity and
awareness. I believe that we can all pick up on other
people's emotions, and sometimes physical pain too.
This type of empathic sensing comes from the aura and
not the body. During your spiritual development you'll
start to become more aware of this; it'll make spiritual
development much easier to take in and explain much
of the so-called mystery of psychic events.

If you sit in a spiritual circle, it's sometimes good to have
a practice session where you try to tune in on the auric
level with another person from your group. Although
this isn't mediumship, it does help you to build on your
empathic abilities, which in turn helps you to sharpen
your sensitivity and feel the emotional memories
of other people and places. This will only help your
mediumship in the future.

This is one of the exercises I use to help my students
experience the auric field of another person:

Exercise: Sensing the auric energy of another person

This exercise is for people working in pairs. One person sits on a chair while the other stands behind them.

❖ Standing person, encourage your partner to relax, take their mind into the silence and stillness and enter the most balanced state they can.

❖ Gently placing your hands on their shoulders, try to tune in with your mind to their physical energy and just let their body tell you when they are relaxed and at peace.

❖ Then just allow your hands to lift five to seven centimetres (two or three inches) above their shoulders and try to sense the atmosphere around their body.

❖ Be aware of your own emotions and feelings throughout this exercise and try to detect any changes, subtle or otherwise. Can you feel what your partner is feeling right at this moment?

❖ Quietly ask them to recall a time when they felt challenged by life, disconnected from loving experiences and positive feelings.

❖ Be aware of how you feel after this question. Can you feel anything in your body? Are you aware of any emotional memories coming into your mind? What is happening to your hands in the atmosphere around your partner?

❖ After a moment, and any reaction you can register, ask your partner to recall one of the happiest times in their life, a memory filled with joy and love, and allow them to bask in this for a while.

❖ Follow the same procedure of awareness and sensitivity. Be particularly aware of your hands and any movement or change of temperature that might occur. Are they getting hot or cold? Are you getting a different feeling from the last memory?

❖ When you feel the moment is right, ask your partner to take their mind back into the silence and try to sense any change in the atmosphere as they move from happy to balanced.

❖ Now gently place your hands on your partner's shoulders again and slowly bring them back to a fully aware state.

❖ When both you and your partner are fully aware, sit together and discuss what you both felt. They will have gone through an emotional experience and you might have picked up on it. Share with them anything you felt when they went through the various recollections.

❖ It's also good to note how their aura felt to you. Did it seem to be tangible in your hands? If so, then your own aura was very active, because when one source of auric energy comes into contact with another, there's a feeling of presence and physical contact. (This can also happen when spirits are close to us and we feel them as a physical presence.)

❖ Once you've shared your findings and feelings, change places and repeat the exercise.

It is quite common to feel the aura of another person as something physical in your hands. Some people have described it as a 'magnetic force' around the other person, while others have said it felt 'vibrational and hot', or sometimes 'cold'. Not everyone will see, hear or sense the same things – it is completely individual. Our description of something is often in accordance with our understanding of it.

It's also interesting to note whether you picked up any emotions and how they related to the memories of the other person. If you saw, heard or felt the actual memories, it gives some measure of how empathic you are.

If you can read the invisible energy and memories of the living, then chances are you can be trained to do the same with subtle energy and consciousness that's not in a body.

Reading from the aura

Many people have asked me if I am a psychic or a medium, and obviously I tell them that I am a medium and that I get my information during a reading from the loved ones in the spirit world. But although this is almost always the case, there are many times when I'm working as a medium that I get a vision of something from the recipient's current life situation, and it comes to me not just with a picture, but also a feeling in my gut.

I remember one very clear case of this when a woman in her fifties came to me for a reading. She was hoping to get in contact with her late husband, and though I tried my best, it was one of those times when no matter what I did – try to tune in as normal, hold a picture of her husband or hold a keepsake that belonged to him – nothing worked.

When I finally understood that I wasn't able to make contact with him, I stopped trying and told the lady that this sometimes happened, it was no fault of hers and from time to time a medium might not be able to lift their mind to the point where they could receive messages.

It's better to be honest in situations like this than struggle on. In some ways it's like your old transistor radio that works fine for six days of the week and yet for no reason you know can't get a clear signal on the seventh day. You can move it around and extend the aerial, but if the waveband isn't right, you might as well turn it off and be done with it. That was what it felt like that day.

My sitter told me that she'd had contact with her husband before and that she wasn't really looking for evidence of life after death, but she wanted to ask him a question. During their life together she'd always been able to depend on him to give her the right directions when she found herself in a bit of a quandary and she thought that he might have come through in a reading and done so again. I totally understood this and was sorry that I couldn't help.

We had a cup of tea and she began to speak to me about her situation. I was quite happy to listen. I'd spent over 20 years as a hairdresser, after all; this wasn't the first time I'd listened to someone telling me some of the intimate details of their life.

This lady told me she'd become romantically involved with a man several months before. It had been more than 10 years since her husband had passed and she was trying to move on with her life. She honestly believed that her husband in the spirit world was fine with her new male friend, but something inside her felt a little bit suspicious of him and she couldn't quite put her finger on it.

As soon as she began to tell me about her feelings of uncertainty, I actually experienced exactly the same thing.

I asked her to continue the story and she went to speak, but instead I came out with 'He's asked you to buy him a new car?!' with such certainty that she almost froze on the spot.

I felt compelled to continue and I knew that I wasn't going to stop until the feeling that was building in me had been expelled.

I heard my voice saying, 'You aren't sure of him because he says that he has lots of money tied up in some sort of financial deal and he only wants to borrow the money for the car, but something at the pit of your stomach has prevented you from lending it to him, isn't this so?'

Well, at that point I really believed she'd drop her cup on the floor.

'Oh my God!' she said.

She was looking at me intensely and I felt that she was waiting for me to continue, so I did. In a matter of 30 seconds I told her the man's name and where she'd met him and said that she was to follow her gut no matter what.

I closed my eyes and in my mind I could see what the man looked like. I described him to her and gave her many details about conversations in which he'd promised to marry her in two years. I also came up with other details, more incriminating ones, which she'd suspected but hadn't allow herself to follow up.

At the end of my outburst I knew that this information was coming from the lady's mind and not from her husband in the spirit world. I sensed no presence, but I had picked up psychic information from a person's aura before and I knew how that felt, and in this case I was certain that all of this information had been sitting in the woman's mind, because she was so concerned.

She was quite shocked when I told her how I was getting this knowledge, and she still wondered if it wasn't coming from her husband, but I felt not. It was my understanding that it was probably best for her to get the information from a stranger, as that way it would have more impact. If it had come from her husband through a medium, she might have had doubts about it or not have acted on it.

I did hear the outcome of this story and, as I'm sure you can imagine, no car was bought and the relationship was ended, as she confirmed many of the things I'd told her.

I honestly don't know if her husband couldn't help at that time or maybe wasn't allowed to, but it all turned out okay in the end.

On the next occasion I saw her, I was able to tune in as a medium to her husband and it felt completely different from the psychic episode of before. It was a much more familiar process to me and a less anxious experience in a way.

What this episode did was remind me that all mediums are psychic, even if we don't always have to use that faculty because normally it's all made easy for us by the spirit friends who come through to their loved ones.

Reporting without fuss

I mentioned earlier that there are people who become connected to the atmosphere of places or buildings when they first encounter them. This is auric sensitivity at work. It shows us that memories can be held in the aura of a place, in its very atmosphere. A true sensitive will be able to access them and report on them without fuss.

It's important that you learn early on that what's happening in the unseen energy around you needn't affect you either positively or negatively. A good sensitive, like a good medium, will feel things and report on them. That's all. They won't adopt them or take them home with them. This kind of thing only happens when the sensitive or medium isn't properly developed and doesn't understand how to disconnect from the old emotion of a situation.

I watched with horror once as a medium stood on stage and attempted to give a message to a couple in their forties who'd lost a son in what sounded like a very tragic accident. She fished for information rather than gave it, so I knew that she wasn't that confident and hadn't trained to the correct standard to be working in public. The other obvious thing that caught everyone's attention was how emotional she became when trying to give the message. In fact there was a moment when she looked far more disturbed than the recipients, and just for a second I honestly thought that the father was going to get out of his seat and go to this emotional wreck and comfort her.

This type of behaviour told us that the person behaving as the medium had more need for support and comfort than the couple who had lost their child.

If you ever see this kind of emotional display from a medium, it's either because they aren't really a medium, or because they haven't had proper training in how to work with the public, or because they haven't any real connection to the spirit world. If only people knew that the spirits who work with us only want to heal and help people, not upset them with silly dramatic and emotional displays.

If you're serious about developing mediumship, you won't want to attract attention to your gift for the wrong reasons, so drama and attention-seeking won't concern you. The true student of mediumship will never add to its mystery, but will always work to lift hearts and minds to higher understanding.

· · · ·

Knowing that you have an extended light body or aura will help prepare you for the next step on our course. When you understand that you're using this type of awareness to pick up information as a psychic or sensitive, you'll be ready to tune your own frequency to a higher level and sense the more subtle energy of the spirit world.

The old proverb 'when the student is ready, the teacher will appear' is one I've used many times, but it's true for all that. If you've managed to get to the point where you're happy to sit in your own quiet mind, you're comfortable sitting in the power of your own auric field and you understand that this inner light is your activated sixth sense, you're ready to take the next step.

This will take you to your true teacher, your spirit guide.

Chapter 4

THE CALLING CARD

'Does everyone have a spirit guide?' This is the question I've been asked more than any other when it comes to my work as a spiritual teacher. The answer I give is the only one I can, and that is, 'Yes, most definitely.'

Spirit guides and guardians

So many people in this physical world want to believe that there is a spiritual being watching over them somewhere out there in the vast universe. It's easy to understand why they want to feel part of that bigger picture. If they knew that a spiritual guardian was guiding them from a higher place, instead of shrinking into insignificance when looking at the mighty heavens around them they might feel part of a more omnipotent force, full of purpose, potential and direction.

Mediums have always felt connected to spiritual teachers or guides from the ascended world of the spirit. I say 'mediums', but in that I include the shamans of the old cultures who would raise the vibration of their mind to talk to their ancestors or higher spirits to get guidance for their people. To all intents and purposes, they were the origin of what we call mediums today.

What I'm saying is that mediumship is a very old practice. Although Spiritualism, which was born in the middle of the 19th century and became a religion in Great Britain in the early 1950s, seems to be what many people associate with the practice of mediumship, it has really been around a whole lot longer than that.

Throughout the history of humanity there have been reports of people with the ability to talk to spirits or see visions and hear the voices of the departed. One thing common to them all, from any time, past or present, is that they talk of a guiding force. Joan of Arc had her council of saints who spoke to her and guided her mission. In the Bible there are many examples of holy men being visited by angelic beings who brought guidance from a higher level and so on. The same thing appears, in various forms, in most, if not all, cultures.

The thing is, guardians and spirit guides don't only belong to the sacred and holy – everyone who is incarnated in this world has a 'spiritual reflection' in the higher realms. This is their guide. Though some people are born instinctively knowing this, everyone can get to know their guide if they know how, and by this I mean if they *really* know how!

In the first development circle that I attended there were so many people who invented an archetypal figure for a guide, like a Native American chief or a religious or holy person from Christianity, and so on. None of them seemed to have been ordinary people before they took up the role of spirit guide. Let's see, we had John the Baptist and Mary, Queen of Scots, to name just two.

Historical figures like this just represent a type – the Baptist a great seer and prophet, for example, and Mary an innocent victim held in a tower. They aren't an indication of what the person's real spirit guide is like, more of where they are psychologically. If the person carries on with their development, though, they will come to learn something from the particular archetype they have chosen. They may even come to know their real guide.

One of my students, Steven, who now works with me, went through the experience of adopting an archetypal spirit guide only to find, several years later, that it was all just a lesson and his true guide was the opposite of his initial vision in almost every respect.

By the time that Steven came to me for help with his development he already had a strong idea of his spirit guide, as mediums had given him messages that suggested he had a Native American watching over him.

As he now admits, after being told this it became easy for him to create such an image in his imagination when he was meditating. No sooner had he tried this than a suitable picture formed in his mind: a proud Native American sitting on a white horse dressed in all the usual garb and so on.

Steven then took this further and asked this image if he was his guide. In his own head he heard a voice say, 'Yes.'

He took it further still and asked the guide if he had a name. Once again a voice in his head answered him, saying, 'Crazy Horse.'

So Steven took this to be the name of the guide. The only thing he wasn't really sure of was whether the voice in his head was coming from the spirit guide or from himself.

At the time he wasn't sitting in a regular circle and his only spiritual practice was when he attended seminars in places like the Arthur Findlay College in Stansted, UK, where budding mediums can go for lessons on how to develop mediumship. Other than these week-long seminars, he was meditating on his own at home with no teacher, so by the time he

*came to me his head was crammed with confusion
and he had no idea what was real and what was his
imagination.*

It is for this very reason that I encourage all my students to take notes at the end of development sessions, but to ignore any images that flood into their mind when they first start to ask about guides. When we put out a question such as this from our mind, it's normal to want to visualize the answer and maybe influence it with desire. I know that I saw many images in my mind during my early meditations, and if each one was a guide I'd honestly have a collection of every historical archetype from Atlantis onwards. It's far better if you can work towards trying to sense the atmosphere around you and pick up any sign of a presence close to you. For me, it was never so much *seeing* that fed my belief in a spirit guide, it was more *feeling* the presence of spirit.

I had, however, already met my guide. When I was a small boy around the age of four or five, I remember seeing a little blonde-haired girl of the same age as me in my bedroom at night. Sometimes this child would be the last thing I'd see before I fell asleep. There were times when I'd be uncertain or even afraid of the things that were happening around me, as all children are at some point, and this beautiful little girl would bring a sense of peace and serenity that would immediately relax me.

I know that many children report seeing imaginary friends. It makes me wonder just how imaginary they actually are. I'm not saying that every child who claims they have an imaginary friend is seeing a spirit being; I just know what happened to me and how it was explained to me as I went through my own development.

Several years into my spiritual journey, I was in a development circle with a group of like-minded friends and had the chance to sit with a great trance medium, or channeller. A trance medium is one who goes into a trance state where they give up some of their conscious mind to the spirit who wishes to speak through them, and allow their spiritual guide to use their faculties.

I was told by this trance medium's guide that my own guide would soon make himself known to me and that I should recall that when I was a child he had chosen to show himself to me as a girl child of the same age, as it was more suitable for a child to see that image than one of an older person from a different culture. The guide went on to give an exact description of the blonde-haired child and the effect her presence had had on me, and I know that I'd never shared that information with another living soul.

It actually made great sense to me that the spirit world, which is very wise and compassionate, would approach a small child like this, as it wouldn't in any way scare me or make the experience feel paranormal, and it didn't, ever.

My guide did reveal himself to me shortly afterwards, just as the trance medium's guide had said, but before I reveal how and why to you, I'd like to explain how I reached this point in my progression.

The calling card of the spirit guide

By now I was several years into my development and was learning to trust the process that Mrs Primrose was teaching me. She was advising me to trust my feelings more than the images that appeared in my thinking mind or the internal conversations I heard. By this point I'd become much more sensitive to the atmosphere around me and when I was sitting in my class I could actually feel when a spirit being was in my auric field. Sometimes it felt as though someone was standing beside me and if I opened my eyes and turned my head I would have seen a person there, although I never did open my eyes.

There was one particular presence that I knew instinctively was my guide. Each time I felt this presence beside me I'd also have the overwhelming sense that fine wispy hair was forming around my mouth and chin, but it didn't feel like my own hair, it felt as though it belonged to someone else. I came to understand that this sensation was my guide's personal way of introducing himself to me and that the facial hair had been a distinct feature of his when he'd last been incarnate in the physical world. He was giving me a sign by which I would recognize him whenever I sat in my class or worked spiritually. It was his calling card, if you like.

How might you recognize the calling card of your own guide?

Exercise: Looking for the calling card

Begin this practice as you normally would with the meditation you've used to this point:

◆ Sit as straight as your body will allow and place your feet flat on the floor to ground yourself.

◆ Relax your shoulders and take a deep breath into your body. Feel your chest expand with this in-breath and then drop as you slowly begin to allow the breath to leave your body.

◆ Become aware of the relaxation that takes over as your body begins to feel peaceful and still.

◆ Allow your breathing to become more natural now that your body is in a state of peace and stillness.

◆ If at any time you are aware of thoughts passing through your mind, just let them move through. Don't hold on to them. Just let your mind relax and sit in the stillness and peace of your own energy.

◆ Be aware that your energy isn't just within your body but is beaming out into the atmosphere around you like a light. Allow your light to expand and glow.

❖ Send out a welcome to your guide, who is out in the atmosphere around you.

❖ Just allow your guide to be in your sacred space.

❖ See if you can feel any sensation or feeling of presence in the energy around you. Just take note of what it is. Don't allow your mind to begin to think or imagine anything, just observe any sense of presence or feeling in your aura.

❖ If there is anything that stands out, ask your guide if they are causing this and wait to see if it intensifies. You may even ask them to remove it and bring it back. Wait for a response.

❖ Now take a deep breath and allow your guide to move out of your light as you begin to bring your awareness back to yourself.

Bring yourself back as you normally would and take a moment to reflect on anything you experienced during that practice. If you are part of a circle, share it with your group. If you are sitting alone, write it down in a diary and date it. It's always good to keep records of your spiritual journey. Even things that don't seem important at the time should have some meaning at a later date.

Remember, the purpose of this exercise is to sense presence rather than try to understand it or imagine what it is. I know that it truly helped me in my development.

As I came to know my guide's calling card, I would mentally ask him to remove the sensation from my face to show it was really him, and I would no sooner have sent out the thought than the feeling of wispy hair on my chin would disappear. Then I would ask him to bring it back and of course it would be there again. This feeling became our code. It's one that I still experience today. It tells me that my guide is around me and usually after that something else is given to me – some information or a task to perform.

On one occasion I got a strong sense of the calling card followed by a vision of a dark-haired young man reaching out to an older woman, whom I instinctively knew to be his mother. He was holding a piece of paper in his hand that looked like a letter. Then I heard a voice in my head saying, 'Alan is safe, Alan is free.'

I had no idea what this meant, as I didn't recognize either person in the vision, but I had a strong feeling that it really meant something and I noted that it had happened right after I'd received the calling card from my guide.

It wasn't long before the vision became a reality. Three nights later I was with Mrs Primrose in our healing clinic when a woman who looked like the lady from my vision came to us and asked if she could receive healing from someone.

At this point I was just a trainee healer, but my teacher told me to work with the woman and that she would oversee us. The healing was okay and I could sense warmth and a feeling of peace around the woman, but then I felt my guide again. His calling card told me he was close by and wanted to add something to the healing.

Then I saw and heard exactly what I'd seen and heard during my circle three days earlier, only now I felt impelled to talk about it or somehow unleash it from my inner self.

I finished the healing session quite abruptly and straight away spoke to Mrs Primrose in a whisper, telling her as quickly as I could manage about the vision. She looked at me and told me to tell the woman that the healing was over and conclude things as usual, but when I had, she took the lady into her office and called to me to follow them.

Mrs Primrose explained to the woman that I'd picked something up during my healing session with her and asked her whether she'd like me to explain what it was, as it sounded like a message from someone in the spirit world.

At that moment, I had no nerves or feeling of trepidation about giving this information because I felt the calling card of my guide again and knew that he wanted this to be done.

It turned out that the woman had a son called Alan who'd taken his own life and had left a letter to explain things to her, but she hadn't been able to find solace in his words. She believed that he was stuck somewhere because of how he'd died and she was depressed and mentally exhausted.

When she heard the short message from her son in the spirit world, she told us it was really important to her and she looked much brighter at the end of the message than at the end of the healing.

I got to know her over the next few months, as she attended our church more regularly after that and it was good to see her grow in strength and confidence.

I too began to grow in confidence. This episode made it easier for me to know when to work as a medium and certainly to trust that the calling card was a true sign that the spirit world wanted to work with me.

Even today when I have doubts about certain things in my life, I send out a thought to my guide and ask, 'If you are close, my friend, may I sense the calling card?' Usually in an instant I get the sign.

My experience was of sensing my guide and then receiving a message for someone, and that's the order it should work in. It's always best to wait for the sign from your guide before you try to give messages to people.

It takes time to learn to sense the spirit world properly and to trust what you are picking up. If you wait for your spirit guide to give you a sign that you can trust, the whole process can be made much simpler.

My confused student Steven began to sit with me at a small private circle in my home shortly after I heard his story of how perplexing his development had been up to that point. I had a real sense that he had a true spiritual gift and I was just as certain that he had been influenced by people who really weren't ready to teach this work.

I can still remember how baffled he looked when I offered him the chance to sit and do nothing and said that if he did nothing well, he could stay in my circle. I assume he thought that I'd be teaching him techniques of mediumship for the very advanced. How wrong he would be!

I must admit, though, that when Steven got into the idea of not trying to imagine things or get results for me, his mind really began to expand. Within the first year I could feel the power around him and knew that the spirit world was ready to introduce itself to him in a proper way. Having already experienced this myself, I couldn't wait to see the reaction of my new student when all those years of confusion turned to bliss with the introduction of a simple calling card.

Trusting your guide

Over time, trust builds between you and your guide, and this becomes a true bond when they give you a task that provides proof that what they are telling you is true, as when I passed the spirit message to Alan's mother. It means that there's an intelligence working behind the presence you can feel, and any visions or messages that come with that presence will carry much more weight than random thoughts.

I kept records of what I experienced while sitting in the circle so that I could check the exact details later, and I was always amazed how meaningful my experiences became later on. This was so important to me in terms of trust and it also informed me that my guide seemed to have knowledge of things that hadn't happened yet.

Once I happened to be sitting in my circle when I started to feel the presence of my guide really strongly around me. The calling card was so clear and pronounced that I honestly wanted to wipe the wispy hair from my face, such was the quality of the experience. I knew that something following would be important, so I tried not to lose my mindful state and to be ready to observe what came next.

Next came a stream of images of people and places that I couldn't make out clearly – it was a bit like watching a television that wasn't tuned in properly. Then the focus sharpened and I saw myself standing on a stage before what looked like a lot of people who were all looking at me with a real sense of expectancy, as though they were waiting for me to speak. I saw the outside of a theatre with the name 'Mackintosh' on the wall, then a single orange and then a monkey sitting on a rock. There was also a strong buzzing sensation around me, as there always was when I had a spiritual experience.

Together the pictures meant nothing at the time, but I wrote down everything I saw, heard and felt and dated it in the little diary that I kept for that purpose. Then I left it to see if it would somehow have meaning when the time was right.

Two years later I was asked to work in Gibraltar, where I gave a demonstration of mediumship in the John Mackintosh Hall to hundreds of people, and just before I walked on stage, I looked out of a window into a sparse little garden that faced the back of the hall and I saw a tree that was bare apart for one orange hanging from a branch.

The monkey turned out to be a very prominent symbol of the rock of Gibraltar. Many tourists go to see the amazing and quite cheeky little monkeys there, something I did myself.

It was episodes like this that made me trust my guide and also have patience and wait for the relevance of the information he gave me to make itself known.

The Gibraltar trip was amazing for me because it was the first time I'd worked in a theatre and it was a turning point in my work as a medium. The timing was special too, as it somehow gave me the power to overcome any worries when it came to working in front of large crowds. Being given knowledge of it in advance told me it would be all right on the night. All I really had to do was physically turn up and the spirit world would do the rest.

If you can learn to trust your guide as early on in your development as possible, then your journey will be much easier. It's just a matter of learning the language of spirit.

The language of spirit – sensation and telepathy

For so much of our life we depend on our sight and hearing as well as our other human senses – smell, taste and physical touch – but we aren't told that much about feeling or sensing.

I found that from a very early age I experienced feelings and emotions that my older siblings never seemed to mention or display, as far as I can remember. Being naturally sensitive in this way, I often reacted emotionally to what came to me. When I was as young as four or five, I remember picking up that some adults who had come to visit my parents were upset, and that made me upset too. I always felt connected to other people's sadness or fear, and because of this I'd try to visualize solutions or just wish the people well from the deepest part of my young being. When I was growing up I had no one to tell me how to cope with this type of sensation and I just had to experience it and hope that someday in the future I'd be able to work it out.

If you think you were like this at any point in your life before you started on your spiritual journey it might turn out that you are naturally empathic. You might be sensitive to other people's emotions and even physical pain. If this is the case then you have to learn how to use this ability and not be brought down by it. Some empathic people can be dragged down when they are in the company of depressed people, while others find it hard to be close to people or places where there is physical suffering.

One of the women who started her development at the same time as me found that she couldn't watch the 10 o'clock news because she wouldn't be able to sleep afterwards, as her mind would be full of the sadness and horror going on around the world. She would almost manifest the pain in her own body, her mind was so programmed to connect with the emotions of others. This was something she'd experienced all her life. (It is a misconception that if psychics feel someone's suffering, they are removing it from them. Though this has happened, it doesn't always have this effect.)

The thing that stands out in my mind about this woman is that she could feel *so much* pain, and not just from watching television. Her sensitivity was switched on to suffering, as is the case with so many people like this, because it would seem that this end of the emotional scale gets our attention more than the loving, happy side. Also, being in our healing class meant she was in the thick of things. She often would describe exactly what people were feeling when she was close to them.

For me, this was a revelation, because I could clearly see that a telepathic message was being passed between the sufferer and the empathic person. It suddenly dawned on me that the messages that came through from the spirit world, either from a spirit guide or a loved one, were being passed through the unspoken language of telepathy.

It was just the same when I sensed the facial hair of my guide – I was picking up on his memory of what he'd looked like in that physical body through pure telepathy!

This also meant that the pain I'd experienced when working with patients during my healing sessions was more a kind of telepathic phantom pain than real living pain. Any empathic healer knows that it's quite common to pick up or mirror the pain of their patients. And more often than not, once you experience the pain and realize where it's coming from, it ceases immediately.

Telepathy can and does also work very well between people who have a strong life connection. In my workshops, I've often used long-term partners or others with a strong love bond to show how it works. It's not a matter of thought to thought, rather that the feelings or urges of one person affect the other person. These feelings can, however, sometimes appear in the mind like thoughts. This depends on how good the receiver is or on the strength of the feeling sent out.

On one occasion a couple who had been together for almost 30 years took part in one of my sessions. I asked them to sit in different rooms and then asked the man if he would go into a light meditation and take his mind to a very important memory in his emotional life. He did so immediately and his mind flashed back to the moment when his son was born. That had been before he was with his current partner.

She had no idea what she was to do, but I'd left a piece of paper and a pencil beside her so she might doodle if she got bored. The incredible thing was how quickly she started to draw a baby. And above its head, she wrote, 'It's a boy, it's a boy.'

Although this woman knew that her partner had a son from a previous relationship, she'd never known how he'd felt at the time of his birth. But while she was drawing the baby, she wept slightly into her sleeve. That was precisely what her partner was doing in the other room while he was telling the group about his feelings at the moment of his son's birth, so not only did his partner pick up on a feeling she couldn't see, she actually felt it and reacted accordingly. Now that's what I call telepathy.

Using telepathy

If you would like to know more about telepathy, there are many books on the subject and some very good work has been done in the United States by Professor Gary Schwartz, who has conducted many scientific tests on telepathic subjects and had some very interesting results.

I would urge you to be alert for telepathy when you work spiritually and try to be aware of the source of the telepathic messages you receive. Remember, much of the information mediums and psychics work with is coming from people in this world, so you must learn to understand the mechanics of your mind as it picks up messages telepathically from this world and the next. How do these messages come to your mind? Is it through sight, sound or sense? We will look at all of these in the following chapter.

As you begin to get to know your guide and their calling card, you can start to use the telepathic connection between you to get answers. Your guide wants you to understand this language, so they will help you to expand spiritually each time you work with them. This isn't a process to be rushed, but your guide will be there and will help you.

Eventually Steven gave up the idea of Crazy Horse being his guide and developed patience and the ability to sit in the power and just wait for his real teacher to appear.

I would see his guide's image overshadowing his body and it was so clear to me what sort of person it was, but like a true teacher I said nothing until my student was ready to confirm it.

It was almost two years after he began sitting in my little circle that Steven began to recognize his guide's calling card, which he described as 'a sensation like an electrical charge' running down his cheek.

I never reacted, but told him just to acknowledge it and wait until something else happened. What Steven didn't know was that I could see that there was a very distinct scar-like line running all the way down his guide's left cheek. I also could see that apart from that, this Asian-looking man seemed quite down to earth and ordinary. He gave me his name, which I kept secret until my student came to know it for himself.

The upshot of all of this was that one evening Steven had an experience in which his whole being lit up. Not only did he feel the calling card of his guide, he felt the whole person. He didn't need visions or imaginings any more, because it was clear that the bond had been made between guide and student; in a moment he knew his guide's name and where he had lived on Earth and when. It was like receiving a spiritual download of another being – the type of episode that turns belief into knowledge and certainty.

I knew that Steven was ready to work more closely with spirit because he'd given up the old ideas that had been put into his mind to impress him and decided to wait for the real thing.

Now, instead of his head being confused and chaotic with doubts and analyses, he was clear and certain and ready to move forwards with total trust, sure that the best was yet to come.

Chapter 5

THREE FACULTIES
OF MEDIUMSHIP

THREE DAUGHTERS
OF MOTHERSHIP

How do you receive your information from the spirit world – by seeing, hearing or sensing? It's important that you start to recognize how your mediumship actually functions so that you can take it further.

Clairvoyance

The word itself only means 'clear vision', but its connotations are more mystical and otherworldly. *Clairvoyance* is the French word the world has adopted to describe the function of seers, fortune-tellers, mediums and any other visionaries who claim to see through time, the spirit realms or the lives of others.

I've observed and worked with clairvoyants, seers and fortune-tellers for more than 30 years now and I've heard some amazing predictions, both good and bad. Some have happened, some haven't.

A friend of mine named Karla is a very good seer, someone I would trust if she came to me with information about a vision she'd had concerning my life or life in general. The reason I trust this lady is because her record of getting hits with her predictions has been very good and many people I know who have used her services as a seer would say the same.

I had an amazing episode with Karla some years ago when I had a bit of dilemma going on in my workplace. People asked me why I didn't ask the spirit world for answers, but this is something I never do for myself. There are many ways to get answers from your life's journey and I often find that if I take the problem into my own meditation, answers will be revealed to me, maybe in a symbolic fashion. Similarly, answers have come to me in a dream state. There have also been times when answers have not forthcoming. We all have to live out certain experiences in our lives without guidance in order to truly understand them. So sometimes answers come through; other times they don't. I've sat with clairvoyants and received nothing. When this happens, I know that I have to find the answers myself through experience.

This time, I tried to tune in to my own future during my meditation to see if I could get an answer, but I got nothing, so for about two months I was in a very difficult place at work. I wasn't enjoying working for my boss and wanted to leave, but he was a friend and I wasn't sure how to change my circumstances without hurting him or making my own life more pressured.

I remember going to Karla's little office for a book I was looking to buy, and when I entered she didn't greet me in her usual friendly manner, but instead stared right through me, as if she was in a trance of some kind.

I remember looking at her and wondering what was going on and if there was something wrong with her. Even though I knew she was a fortune-teller, I'd never seen her do this before.

I stood as frozen as she was for about a minute, which seemed a long, long time. Then, she spoke to me, though her eyes were still fixed on the wall behind me.

'You are worried about your job and you don't have to be.'

These were the only words to leave her mouth and break the silent pause we shared.

Then she appeared to be present again and she looked me up and down for a second or two before adding, 'One week from now you will leave your job amicably and no one will be upset. Now you have to trust me and stop concerning yourself about it.'

That was it and my friend was back to being my friend again.

'So how can I help you today, Gordon?'

It was as though nothing out of the ordinary had happened.

I bought my book from her little collection of spiritual books for sale, we exchanged pleasantries and chitchat about family and I went back to work with the news that all would be well in one week.

Of course she was bang on, as she'd been many times before. The following week one of my boss's friends asked him if he could recommend a hairdresser to take over a salon in another part of town and he asked me if I'd be interested, as he felt I was ready to manage my own salon and that this was a great opportunity.

So I was able to leave without upsetting him and the uncomfortable feeling I had about not enjoying my work in his salon never needed to be broached. All was well, as Karla had predicted, and she'd done it without prompting – it had just come to her.

I've also had my share of visions in my time – lucid dreams that came to pass and visions of events that happened the following day. These were things that were important to me or my family, never big disasters or world-changing episodes.

I believe that everyone has inner visions of some sort. We all have the capacity to make mental images of thoughts and memories, and we all dream.

On your mediumship journey, when you sit in the silence, try to be aware of any images that appear in your mind. Take the time to observe what types of thoughts try to pull your attention away from your quiet practice. Try not to assume that every vision that comes into your mind is a message; it takes time and practice to know the difference. Sometimes your own memory will throw up images and it's important that you learn to know the difference between your own thinking and any clairvoyance that might happen during your sessions.

First, you might find that your thinking is still very connected to the events and situations that are going on in your immediate life, for example, pictures of the day you've just spent with friends and family, or concerns that you've pushed away but know you have to deal with, or images of things you would like to happen to you or your loved ones.

I've come to learn that real clairvoyance is given when the moment is right. If, like me with my situation at work, you get no answer to questions you ask during your meditation, then take that as a no, or that it isn't time for you to know yet. Sometimes things have to happen in order for a better answer to be given. For me, there obviously wasn't a clear vision to be given when I tried myself, but when I stood in the company of a friend who was a natural seer, the circumstances were right to find the answer through her gift. To me, it honestly didn't matter *where* that answer came from, but the fact that it did come eased my mind.

The message that Karla gave to me was very spontaneous and exact, but don't worry if you don't get clear clairvoyance like this at the beginning – this lady was a seasoned professional. Learn from those who are good at their craft, but never try to emulate them; always take your time and proceed slowly at the beginning. Karla isn't a medium and is happy to state that she never will be, but she is a great clairvoyant who has built her gift through practice and dedication.

Take note of your abilities. If you are clairvoyant, observe how you see the images in your mind. Are they clear and distinct or fuzzy and blurred? Are they in black and white or colour? Remember, clairvoyance isn't given to you by a spirit guide or guardian – they merely use what's available to work with. So, if your mind is like a television screen, is yours a small black-and-white one or a large HD colour one, with all the intricate graphics? What do you have to offer? Does your inner screen need to be tuned a little to clear the picture and improve the images?

When I first started to develop, I had the natural ability to sense and hear the spirit world, but I found that the images in my mind were dull and grey. So when I made a link to my guide I asked him to teach me a skill that would help me to improve this over time. It wasn't that I didn't get episodes of clairvoyance, but they were filled with too many images, symbols and characters that made no sense to me, or even to other people in the circle when I told them about my experiences.

It might help you to know that many students of mediumship have confusing experiences at the beginning of their development. What this indicates is that you aren't as mindful as you need to be to interpret the pictures and messages in your inner world. The same might be said for your everyday life.

If you find that you don't get many pictures, or you do, but they are fuzzy, then be open to practising mindfulness as a way of improving what you see.

Mindfulness

The exercise I was given by my guide to help me to become more mindful was quite simple:

❖   I was told to find a quiet place, like a garden or park, and sit quietly and still my mind as I would in the exercise of sitting in the silence, only with my eyes open.

- Then I had to let my eyes take in the surroundings and observe them, as if I was actually filming the scene with my own sight.

- Once I had observed as much of the scene as I could, I had to allow my eyes to close and try to recreate the picture in my mind.

At the outset I found this very difficult, as I would immediately be drawn to the most prominent feature of the place I was in. It seemed to me that it was easy to take in what was obvious, but the smaller details were lost to my visual intake.

However, the more I took myself off to practise mindfulness, the more I became aware of smaller things, like how the line of the landscape in the park moved up and down from left to right on my immediate horizon and how clusters of bushes that I'd first thought of as a solid green mass of leaves were really yellow, brown, beige and different hues of green.

After a few months of doing this practice I found that my sight was expanding, and not only in the park. I also began to see much more of the everyday world I was living in. Soon it felt like a completely different place. My walk to work each morning seemed like another world. Whereas before I used to notice nothing because I was caught up in my thoughts, now I started to take note of places and buildings, and eventually I realized that I was encountering the same people in the same places each day, and it dawned on me that I was actually becoming present in my own life. No longer was I being pulled into my thinking and letting the outside world pass me by; I was interacting with the world I lived in.

My meditation practices also became much clearer and easier to understand. I realized that my guide had given me another practice that had helped me to clear the clutter from my inner world, which meant that I would find it much easier to take more into my mind and not become confused by the obvious. I would have the sense to see that every bit of fine detail had meaning and purpose – and I would perceive it all.

What was happening on a more spiritual level was that my guide obviously knew that I had the capacity to use my clairvoyant ability to a much greater degree than I was doing when I first went into my development circle. So, rather than putting more confusing messages into my mind, he taught me how to use my visual ability in my everyday life, knowing that it would operate the same way during the sessions of meditation when I linked with the spirit world.

This was the first thing I truly learned about clairvoyance: how to prepare my mind to be tuned, visually aware and mindful. Remember, if you wish to develop your mediumship to the highest level you can, you should prepare yourself to the highest standard that you can.

Clairaudience

This faculty of mediumship works in much the same way as clairvoyance. The clairaudient person hears information or messages from the spirit world or about a person they are reading for. The most famous clairaudient is possibly St Joan of Arc, who claimed to hear what she called her 'spiritual council' of St Michael, St Margaret and St Catherine, who guided her to fight to put the true king of France back on the throne in the 1500s.

In more recent times we had a lovely medium in the UK called Doris Stokes who had many books published on her work as a clairaudient medium and filled theatres around the country and in many other parts of the world. Doris would sometimes openly ask the spirit who was working with her to give names and other information that she could use to provide evidence from the spirit world. I liked the fact that she always told people that it was her spirit guide who was the main communicator and who brought the other spirits to her when they needed to give messages to their loved ones. This is something I believe happens when I work this way.

Many mediums report that they hear the voices of spirits passing messages to their loved ones. I receive many messages in this way and find that when I have a very strong connection to the communicating spirit, the faculty of clairaudience becomes more predominant. I recall reading that Doris Stokes felt exactly the same: when she felt a strong presence, the voices got louder and clearer.

The mindful practice I described earlier was also my way of increasing my awareness of what was audible in the world around me. In the early sessions, my mind was overtaken by the sound of traffic on the roads or dogs barking nearby, but after many sessions I honestly began to hear the sound of light winds moving through the trees, bushes and grass, and even more subtle sounds like small branches softly creaking in the distant trees, sounds I knew I could never hear outside my mindful practice.

This practice also increased my clairaudient awareness. I do believe that I was born with clairaudience, but if you want to be better at your craft you should be open to expanding even that which is natural to you. Those born with music or art at their fingertips get even better when they practise, for example.

Being mindful of your hearing will also help you to listen to the people who will come to you when you are eventually working as a medium or healer or spiritual counsellor.

I remember one time hearing my guide tell me that if I wanted to hear the truth of what people were saying then I should become more attuned to the sound they made rather than the words they said. I totally understand this – much more now than when it was first said, in fact. A lot of truths can be heard in the sounds we make, even if our words are suggesting something else.

I've come to learn that a medium who wishes to improve their spiritual gifts should improve themself first, and I've tried to make myself the best receiver of spiritual messages I can be. Now when I tune in to a person for a reading or to a group before a demonstration, I open my senses to their full capacity in both worlds and my senses of vision and hearing are waiting to receive as soon as I feel the spirit presence. Which brings us to clairsentience.

Clairsentience

Clairsentience is the ability to sense spirits who are trying to communicate with us. Rather than seeing or hearing them, we feel their presence in the atmosphere around us, using the auric awareness we talked about earlier.

Sensing in this manner can be practised in a circle with our guides or as part of an exercise such as tuning in to another person's auric energy (*see page 52*), which helps us to strengthen our ability to sense subtle messages in the unseen world around us.

Remember, there are sensitives who only work on the psychic or intuitive level and this means that their sensitivity only extends to people in this world. That is fine if that is to be where your gift works best.

A medium, however, might find that as their ability to sense becomes more acute, they start to feel things like the actual personality of the communicating spirit or the sensations of emotional episodes in their life, both good and bad.

I believe that becoming more sensitive to the emotional and atmospheric activity around us is equally as important as improving our other faculties of mediumship, if not more so. One of the best ways to improve your clairsentience from the very outset is to attempt to link with your guide when you are in circle, as explained in the last chapter.

Understanding how your gift works

It is important to understand more about the process of what is happening for you, so that you can understand how best to improve your own gift.

Observing your own mediumship

The next exercise is very simple and allows you to observe how you receive your information from the spirit world. You may experience clairvoyance, clairaudience and clairsentience all in one session, or two of the three. Is there an order to the process or is it random? How does it work for you?

Exercise: Being mindful of your mediumship

❖ In your circle or your own sacred space, begin as normal by taking your mind into the silence.

❖ Be aware of the atmosphere around you and notice how still and quiet it is.

❖ Be aware that your energy isn't just within your body, but is beaming out into the atmosphere around you. Sense the vibration in your own energy as it expands outwards in all directions from your body.

❖ Send out a thought to your spirit guide and welcome them into your sacred space.

❖ Allow your awareness to sense the presence of your guide and whatever signals you have come to know and accept.

❖ When you are truly aware of your guide and are satisfied that you are connected, ask if you may receive information about the life they led when last in the physical world.

❖ Wait to see if it is given. Be aware of anything that comes to you (and also aware that you aren't forcing it).

❖ Watch for pictures. This is an indication that your clairvoyance is working.

❖ It is the same for words or sounds – those are an indication of clairaudience. Are you hearing anything?

❖ Check your feelings and any sensations around your physical being. Note anything that feels different on both the physical and emotional level.

❖ When you are satisfied, thank the guide and allow them to move out of your space.

❖ Bring yourself back in the usual way and when you feel ready, note down anything that you saw, heard or felt after you asked your guide for information.

It's good to try exercises like this to see if you are picking up information from your guide. Remember, if you can do this with your spirit guide, then as you progress, you can do it with other spirits who wish to work with you.

In the early stages of your development, though, it's important that you don't get too bogged down with the mechanics. Try to take time to let things unfold rather than blast your brain with too much at one time. Remember, once you have a link to your guide, understanding will come to you when you're ready. Your guide will always regulate what you need (rather than what you want).

Sometimes, through all this development, you will have lots of sensitive experiences. For instance, there may be times in your everyday life when your sensitivity awakens you to emotional situations around you. When such things occur, try to react in the same way you would in meditation and, linked with your spirit guide, try to see such situations for what they are. Just because you can feel other people's emotional chaos doesn't mean you have to react to it. Just observe and process what you're picking up.

During my development, for example, when I was working closely with a client in the hairdressing salon, I would sometimes sense that there was something deeper going on beneath what they were telling me. But, as they weren't asking me to help them as a sensitive, I never felt obliged to share what I was picking up.

Mrs Primrose always said that spiritual development caused us to become much more sensitive in everyday life, but we always had to maintain boundaries when people weren't asking for our help or advice. Being sensitive means that you may feel many things that others can't; a disciplined sensitive will always know when to observe or react.

If at any time things are developing too quickly for you, simply stop and have a little break from your spiritual work and ground yourself by doing everyday activities – walking the dog, digging the garden, cleaning the car and so on. When there's too much happening in the mind, it's time to touch the Earth.

Psychometry

Another good exercise for building your abilities and understanding how your gift works is psychometry. This is an old practice used by mediums and psychics and it involves tuning in to an object that belongs to someone and trying to get a reading from the vibrational energy attached to it. All physical objects have a vibrational energy and a psychic may sometimes sense this and describe feelings and pictures associated with the history of the object or people and situations that have influenced it.

Exercise: Reading the vibes

This is a particularly good exercise if you sit with a group of people, as you can all try it at the end of your meditation practice. It is very easy to do.

Each sitter should privately place a personal object into an envelope at the beginning of the session. Then each should choose an object from the envelope to begin the exercise. (Make sure it belongs to one of the other sitters.)

❖ Hold the object, clear your mind and still your thinking to the best of your ability.

❖ Just wait until you see images or feel any type of sensations emotionally or around your body.

When I was first asked to try this in my circle with Mrs Primrose, I'd never done this before, so I'd no idea that anything would happen at all, but my teacher felt that I was at a point where I could expand my mental practices, so I went along with it.

Several of us were asked to choose an object from a basket that contained things like rings, watches and necklaces, all of which had been gathered together by Mrs Primrose earlier. Once we'd chosen the object we were drawn to, we had to close our eyes and clear our mind and then just talk about what we were experiencing while holding the object.

A lady sitting next to me started by saying that she was experiencing a lot of heat in her hand and was seeing a small woman to whom she felt her object belonged. She gave a description of this lady and then she said that she felt that this woman had died several years before and that she'd worked as a healer in life, as the heat she kept feeling in her hand increased several times when she saw a picture in her mind of the woman putting her hands on people in the fashion of a healer.

She was correct in everything she said – the object belonged to one of Mrs Primrose's friends, who had resembled the description given, had been a healer in Mrs Primrose's church, and yes, had passed away.

Now it was my turn to speak and I squeezed my object tightly in my hand. It was a locket on a gold chain. I instantly saw a vision in my mind of a young man of about 18 years of age who was wearing a tracksuit and a white baseball cap. I said this out loud and my teacher nodded her head in agreement.

I then had a feeling in my stomach, a kind of sick feeling. I felt that I was ill, that I couldn't eat anything, as I was sure that I wouldn't be able to keep it down.

I described the feeling I was experiencing and once again my teacher nodded her head in agreement.

I then heard a voice inside me saying, 'John.' There was a pause and then I heard it again.

Each time I verbalized it and my teacher nodded to me again.

I thought I'd finished, but then I began to speak spontaneously and said that John was the boy I was seeing and that he'd died of a cancer that had made him feel very sick and that I was certain that his picture was in the locket I was holding and was equally sure that this item was his mother's and that she was a friend of Mrs Primrose's.

At the end of my spontaneous outburst my teacher thanked me and told me that everything I'd said was correct and she was happy with the reading I'd got from the object.

I remember thinking that it was quite something to hold an object you'd never seen before and extract information from it, but it was explained to me and the others that this practice was one of the first that Mrs Primrose gave to her students to see if they had any clairvoyant, clairaudient or clairsentient abilities.

I'd seen a picture of the young man and then I'd felt his illness and then I'd heard a voice saying his name, so I'd experienced all three of the elements of mediumship in one go. Other people did the same that night and it was also clear to hear when someone spoke only of seeing, hearing or sensing.

I thought that it was very clever of my teacher to give us this exercise and then observe us. For her, it was a clear way to see where her students were headed in their development, and it is something I use today when I work with new people, as it helps me to work out where they are currently and what I might do to help them understand their gifts.

Psychometry is also good for students who don't have a circle to sit in. If you're developing on your own, you can still ask people to give you an object to tune in to and at the end of your meditation you can just sit with it and see what comes to you by way of pictures, feelings, words and so on. Write everything down and tell the owner at a later date. Take feedback, as it will help you to measure your progress.

An old practice like psychometry can sharpen your sensitivity and also help you to learn how to do a reading for someone. I suppose my first experience of psychometry was the first actual reading I did whilst under the guidance of my teacher, and when I'd finished I remember I wanted to do it again, but I was told that I shouldn't just go out and do it for everyone I met, as I'd eventually confuse myself and burn my gift out. Mrs Primrose was a great one for patience. She believed, as I now do, that at first these things should only be done when we were in our spiritual class and that we should wait until we were more experienced before pouncing on the general public.

It would be my advice to try psychometry as part of your development and when you see that you are getting a good hit rate time and again, then you can try it on friends and eventually progress to people who want a reading from you. Even then, it's always wise to tell people that you are still developing your gift.

Making notes

I've said it before, but it's good to note down all of your experiences. As you proceed, it will help you to see how your gift is shaping up.

The other thing about keeping records of your progress is that you'll be able to recognize any changes in your meditation as they happen.

There will also be times during a practice like psychometry when you get things that don't mean anything, yet several months, or in some cases years, later you might find an answer that wasn't there at the time.

I remember when I was sitting in the second of the development circles in my life, we were fortunate enough to have a woman in our group who drew the things she picked up during our sessions. This is referred to as 'psychic art' and this woman, my friend Dronma, is one of the best in that field. At the end of the circle she'd share her drawings with the rest of the group and we'd all be fascinated by the way she'd drawn images of things that the rest of us had been getting during our meditations.

One evening, for example, one of the group had said that she'd experienced a vision of a Catholic nun who was wearing a white habit and looked as though she was very young. Dronma was able to show her a picture she'd drawn of a young novice dressed in a habit that matched the description exactly. This type of thing was common in that circle.

The last drawing that Dronma displayed that night was of a dog, but no one in the circle had any connection to the animal and none of us could say we'd picked it up during our session. What would happen when no one had a connection to a drawing was that Dronma would date it and keep it for future reference.

Nine months later I was asked if I would take in a rescue dog that had been very badly treated. As a dog-lover, all I have to do is look at a helpless animal to feel compelled to rescue it, and that's exactly what happened here.

The week after, I took the dog into my circle. All of us loved him: we loved it when he fell asleep while we meditated and bounced around when we came out of our practice. But it was only when Dronma began to show her drawings to the group that someone said, 'Doesn't this dog look a bit like the one that came through in the circle some months ago?'

We all looked at our psychic artist and she started to pull back the pages of her pad until she found the drawing. It was quite remarkable, because not only had she drawn the correct breed of dog, a springer spaniel, but she'd even shown details of his collar and the ornate little barrel he'd been wearing around his neck when I'd got him.

This wasn't the end of the story either, as we checked the date of the drawing and it was

8 December 1995. This was the actual date that my dog was born. The reason I knew this off the top of my head was that the day before the circle I'd been sent his paperwork by his previous vet and his date of birth was on it. And there it was on Dronma's art pad.

So you see it's really important that you record everything that happens in your development sessions. No matter how trivial it might seem, chances are that it came to your mind, or someone in your circle's mind, for a reason. Though it may not have any meaning at the time, remember there's no time in the spirit world and also that mediumship can work across time, so record all your experiences, as you never truly know when they will be helpful to you or someone else in your circle.

Demonstrating in the power

Spirit communication happens when the mind can get out of the way and the amazing power of spirit can work in each and every way – clairvoyantly, clairsentiently and clairaudiently. When you get to the point where you don't care how it works, you just know that it does, you are truly working in the power of spirit. It is at this point that you know that all the years of preparation and development have been worthwhile.

Recently I was working in Germany, in the beautiful medieval town of Regensburg in Bavaria, when I was asked to give a public demonstration of mediumship in the town hall. The event was quite well attended and many of the students from my workshop brought their partners and other family members.

When I work in Germany I'm always accompanied by an interpreter, as my German is very limited and also it is better for the audience to hear everything clearly in their own language. The interpreters I work with regularly tell me that once they begin to translate my words, they often feel that they are connected to me and even begin to visualize what I'm saying, especially if I'm working clairvoyantly.

That particular evening began with me giving a short talk to prepare the audience for what might take place. Talks like this are especially helpful for people who have never seen a medium work and also for those who are doubtful or even sceptical about life after death. I also like to give an introduction to my work because it puts people's minds at rest when I explain that there's nothing mystical or spooky about it, that it will mainly consist of me getting information and passing it to the audience, that at worst it will feel like a conversation between the two worlds and that I'm merely the reporter.

The other reason mediums speak to their audiences before they start to work is so that they can build the power around them and tune in to the spirit world. It's very difficult to start a demonstration cold and the short talk helps to create a sense of relaxation until the energy is at the correct pitch to link with the spirit world.

On this particular evening I remember that my first contact went to a man sitting at the back of the audience. I began by telling him that his father was with me, that he was called Mr Müller and that he had passed three years earlier from a heart attack, all of which the recipient understood quite clearly.

In this case I had begun by sensing the presence of the spirit man, so there was an element of clairsentience at work, but then I'd heard his name being spoken right by my ear, which told me that there was also an element of clairaudience working. Then I went on to describe what the man looked like when he was young and gave many other details about places he'd lived in during the course of his life on Earth. So clairvoyance became the most prominent faculty at the end of the message.

During a public demonstration, the medium isn't really concerned about how the information comes to them. When they're working, the whole thing just feels very spontaneous and natural. I honestly don't have many thoughts in my head about what's happening, especially when I feel the power getting stronger; it feels like working from inside a bubble of electric energy that's being controlled from a remote place above me.

Back in Regensburg, my recipient seemed to be very happy with his message from his father on the other side. For me, a first contact like this in a demonstration helps to build the power and make the connection much stronger for the next contact.

As the power grew, I felt myself being turned to my right and I picked out a man in his late thirties in the front row. He was sitting with his arms folded across his chest and a stern look on his face – the very picture of scepticism and disbelief. As I spoke to him, he sat up straighter in his seat and his look hardened into one of defiance.

I immediately heard the voice of a woman telling me that she'd recently passed from cancer and I heard the word 'mother' being spoken very clearly next to my left ear. Once again I was working clairaudiently, and this carried on for most of the message. This woman was indeed the man's mother and when she told him off for making a parachute jump the week before, I believe that he had no option but to assume that I was getting personal knowledge from somewhere that he couldn't understand.

By the end of the message, his mouth was open and he was on the edge of his seat with one hand on his chin and the other in front of his heart. The message was obviously very personal and very moving for him. As for me, I just reported the details that were given to me, and because it was almost all clairaudience, it appeared very quick-fire and to the point.

As the evening progressed, I heard the names of German streets and places that were completely unknown to me. I just passed them on and my interpreter looked a little shocked, because he hadn't heard of some of the places either. He seemed amused by how well my pronunciation came out.

At the end of the demonstration he told me that as the messages had become stronger and clearer, he could have sworn that he was actually hearing the same information at the side of his head as I was. He also reported that several times he'd seen images of the spirit people I was describing. He was wondering how this could have occurred.

I explained that because he was standing beside me, he was in the same bubble of power as I was. He wasn't the first interpreter I'd worked with who'd told me they'd felt connected to the mediumship.

At the end of that night in southern Germany, many people came to speak to me and ask how I could know the names of obscure German streets and places. Others wanted to know how I could hear the names and describe so accurately how and where people had lived and died.

But the most important conversation I shared that night was with the man whose mother had come through. He told me that he'd been a complete sceptic when he'd come to the town hall, but not only had he received evidential information, but there had been a moment when he'd felt his mother's presence as I was talking. So now he knew there really was life after death.

For any medium, this kind of message really helps to strengthen your confidence in the spirit world and it shows that trust is one of the strongest elements required to work in public like this. All of the technical details can be worked out in development circles, but on the night you have to work in the power, trust and let go. If you can do this, many people will be helped and may even change their view on life.

Mediums will often call themselves clairvoyants and so on. But, for me that only matters after the work is done. I believe that if you develop properly then all the faculties of mediumship can be brought out in you when you work in the power and trust your spirit guide to bring the messages.

Chapter 6

WORKING
IN CIRCLE

Sitting in a spiritual circle has been a big part of my life, as I've been doing it for more than 30 years, more than half of my lifetime to this point.

I recently chatted with a young medium who couldn't believe that I was still sitting in my circle after all this time. He told me that he'd been in a circle for a year and that he felt that was long enough to learn what he needed from the spirit world. He is only one of many who share this opinion. I, on the other hand, have never felt that my development has come to an end. I believe that it will go on throughout my life, and therefore as long as I am able, I will sit in a spiritual circle.

Looking at what a circle is to a medium, or to anyone who wishes to sit and develop their awareness, the first thing I would say is that it is a place where people of like mind come together, so if ever you are confused or stuck on your path, there is always someone in your circle you can talk to or share things with.

This is great for the spiritual student, because often you are working in very normal nine-to-five situations where people never have conversations about spiritual things, or you are part of a family that doesn't understand your beliefs. It can be very difficult if you don't have people to share things with.

One of the healers in Mrs Primrose's church would come to our healing clinic every Tuesday night, and at first I never noticed that he always came with a sports bag in his hand; it was only after we'd chatted that he told me that his family all believed that he went to a gym each week for a couple of hours. I suppose you could say that the healing he did was a kind of spiritual workout!

He once told me that he'd been a practising healer for 40-something years and his wife and children had never known anything about his other life. He told me that he was never able to sit in a circle as he didn't want to commit to something that he knew he couldn't truly dedicate himself to.

This man reminded me that the dedication and devotion a person has to have when they make this commitment to spirit has to be total or not at all. I am happy to make that commitment and continue to sit in a circle and link to the spirit world for guidance and learning. I am still learning new things each time I sit with that great source. I hope that in the future I can share more about the most recent teachings and phenomena from the spirit world, but we are at the very beginning of our journey here, so it will have to wait. But I think it's good to say that even after 30-odd years of linking with my guides in circle there's certainly still a lot to learn and some great new stuff coming through that excites us all.

Open and closed circles

The first circle I ever sat in, at Mrs Primrose's spiritual church in Glasgow, was open to the public, so it was what is known as an 'open' circle, as opposed to a private group where you can choose whom you sit with, which is a 'closed' circle. This meant that each week you might have new people coming in, though in all the years I attended there was always a core of people like myself who turned up every week.

Like all things, an open circle has its positives and negatives. For me, the positive thing about it is that you get to meet all sorts of people, and though this might sound chaotic, it's always good to work with new energy. An open circle seems to have a sense of movement rather than stillness, but, as my teacher would say, 'Spirit can develop in any situation!'

This is very true, and even though at the time I'd nothing to compare it with, I felt that my first circle was perfect. I didn't seem to notice the changes as people came and went, and because of my regular attendance I found myself becoming part of the core group and we brought a sort of stability to all the motion that went on around us. There was always a sense of family, or at least familiarity, and I believe that this sense of community within a group or circle is what gives it strength. Even in this open circle there was great synergy between the core members and I was very lucky to be accepted into this group.

If you do come across an open development circle on your spiritual journey then you can always have a try to see if it's right for you. Open circles are there so that people can sample the experience before making a deeper commitment.

The other thing with the open circle is that it's normally much larger than a closed or private circle. There were at least 20 of us who always attended Mrs Primrose's circle and there were some weeks when we would have 40 to 50 people there.

If you don't like to meditate in big crowds, this might not be for you, but I'd like to say that even though our open circle was at times really large, I honestly learned so much in that group. I believe that I am a people person and I always liked the different faces turning up now and again.

Another thing I learned from my early development was how to discipline my mind in such a large group. Often there would be people who couldn't settle and would become disruptive during the session, but if you can balance your mind in that sort of situation and not allow your lower thinking to be ignited, then you know that you are in a good inner space.

Recently I was with Steven in Germany and one of our new students told us that she found it very difficult to meditate because she could hear the sound of a clock ticking. I honestly wish she could have sat in our large circle full of hustle and bustle. There were times when you might not have heard a horn being sounded!

The thing about this lady's experience was that she could hear the clock ticking but she hadn't got the mental discipline to use this rhythm to her advantage. It also showed that she was easily irritated when she was in her inner space. That was neither 'right' nor 'wrong', by the way, just her reaction. But a meditator does need to recognize their own reactions and work with them.

The importance of a circle

There are so many lessons to learn about the self on this path. I believe that each opportunity we give ourselves brings its own rewards, and in my first circle my rewards were the many realizations I had and many true friends I met. Six of us went on to start our own private circle after our teacher went to the spirit world and then a very different kind of spiritual development started for us.

For the new student, it's important when you find a circle that you at least give it a go. Many people think that the reason the mediums and healers of old were so good was because of how dedicated they were to their circles and to the spirit world. I have to admit that as my life has gone by I've come to believe this also, as I've watched my share of mediums and healers come onto the spiritual path with great vigour and ambition only to lose their spiritual zest after they don't quite get what they believed they would out of the spiritual life. I think that people who develop in long-term circles seem to have a greater battery life, as it were. In Olympic terms, they might achieve bronze for 40 years rather than gold for one year.

There will always be different opinions, but I think that making a commitment to something like a spiritual group is very important. It's equally important to sit on time every week. I say 'week' because that's how my circle has always worked, but you could have more sessions if you felt the need. I always like to allow at least a week to go by in between sessions so that I can process what has happened in my mind and my life, and I've always felt that you can't cram your mind with spiritual thoughts all the time – that the mind needs to open slowly to new things.

For me, the circle is like a battery of power that helps to boost our signal to the spirit world. It has often felt like a beacon of light that lifts the mind to a more enlightened state.

One of the most important things about a circle is that it should be a place of pure compassion. I often look on my circle as being like the upper triangle in the diagram I gave earlier. The circle is where we find love and goodness, and those qualities get stronger because we always offer to share them with others.

I always think back to the times when Mrs Primrose would teach us that whenever we had a spiritual connection with our guide we should think of someone who needed help or healing, someone we knew or had heard of who was going through a dark time in their life. It was her belief that one of the main things that spirit guides were there to teach us was compassion. At the end of every circle, she would dedicate any energy that had been built by the group to people who were less fortunate than we were. It was such gestures that taught me the value of our circle; it made it feel that we were doing good. That very feeling helps consciousness to lighten and expand.

Development in a circle will always expand the mind and make us more aware of ourselves and of the spirit world around us. We know we live in a world that contains much pain and sorrow, but if we can see things from a higher state of vibration, the way spirits do, we can understand things better and also see how we can make a difference.

My first private circle

When I started my own private circle I had already been developing for seven years. I had been taught how to practise healing by Mrs Primrose and she had helped me to understand and use my mediumship too. As I mentioned before, when many mediums reach this point they feel that they are ready to graduate, as it were, from school, but my development was never like a school to me, it was more a way of life, and I honestly knew that there was much more I could learn.

My first private circle was made up of six good friends. If you wish to start a circle, it's always better if you truly know and trust the people you will sit with, especially if the circle is to be held in your own home, as mine was.

We had decided to come together to try to create a spiritual space where we could build the power to link with our spirit guides. At first we would just sit and join hands, and I would open the circle with an address to the spirit world, a kind of prayer if you like. This type of opening is done to show respect for the spirit world and as a means of focusing all the sitters' minds on the nature of the circle, on bonding with the spirit world.

Once the opening was over we would relax our hands into our lap, quiet the mind, sit in the power and then ask our guides to link with us so that we could feel their power.

During these sessions some of us might get messages for others or pick up information for some of our friends and families. When this type of thing happens, it highlights the people in your circle who are equipped with clairvoyance, clairsentience and so on.

At the end of our new private circle we would all concentrate our thoughts with the intention of sending out healing to wherever it was required – something we'd all learned from Mrs Primrose. Right at the very end we all seemed to find that we'd start to breathe more deeply and in perfect harmony with one another, and it would be the awareness of this synchronized breathing that would bring us back to focus on the room and eventually to open our eyes.

Telepathy

I've mentioned already how important it is in any circle for the group to discuss their individual experiences at the end of the session. If you're sitting with a small circle of friends, you might find that more than one person experiences the same vision or feeling and so on, and if this type of thing starts to happen regularly then it opens up your thinking as to what might be causing it.

Telepathy is once again the answer. This is what is activated when the sitters in a circle start to bond. In my own circle we found that by the end of our first year of sitting, all of us were starting to tune in to almost exactly the same thing each week, and what it showed was how amazing the telepathy between us was becoming.

Remember, telepathy is the language of spirit. What we were learning as a group was that our guides had found a way to teach us all this invisible language. Telepathy is a form of communication that is more about feeling and sensing than words, and it felt as though a spirit would come into the circle and each of us would sense them in our own way. Sandra, who sat on my right, would see them and give a great description of what they looked like, while Christine, who sat next to her, would describe how they felt in terms of the height, weight and so on that they had had when they had been in the physical realm. As for me, I would often hear a sort of conversation inside me that wasn't made up of words, but more feelings of what was being said.

As each one of us gave our information, Jackie would write it down in our circle diary, which was very important to our group.

At the end of a session, our psychic artist, Dronma, would show us her drawings and corroborate our findings with hers. We were so fortunate to have her in our circle.

I'll never forget one night when we were all sitting in my flat in the circle as usual but for some reason there was a feeling of unrest among us. This had never happened in all the years we'd sat together and we all opened our eyes at the same time and looked at one another with strange looks on our faces. It was as if we were waiting for something to happen, and no sooner had we thought that than it did: the doorbell rang loudly.

We realized that it might not have been the best thing for us all to have been sitting in the power when this happened, so there was a great sense of relief among us. At least our telepathy had brought us all back at the same moment.

I remember that the next thing was that we all gave a knowing little smile and looked at Jim, whose job it was to take the battery out of the doorbell and unplug the phone before we began. He'd obviously forgotten to do this.

At that time I lived in the basement flat of a Spiritualist church in Glasgow and the caller must have been trying to speak with someone at the church, which was now closed for the night, so we didn't answer. The doorbell rang a further three times, but we all just went straight back into our circle.

We must have sat for another 15 minutes or so, but there was much less of the power that we would normally sit in. When this happened, as it sometimes did, it was quite usual to pick up on clairvoyance, so I knew it would be interesting to compare notes at the end of the circle.

Sandra started by saying that she'd seen an elderly woman wearing a camel-hair coat and a brightly coloured scarf. She also gave a description of her hair and face and so on.

As we went round the circle it was becoming clear that the woman had connected with all of us. When it came to me, I reported that I'd heard the name 'Mrs Wallace' and then 'Agnes', and I felt these were something to do with the same woman.

It was when Dronma revealed her drawings that we were all totally gobsmacked. She had drawn the woman Sandra had described – a woman with soft, wavy white hair, dressed in a light brown camel-hair coat – only this lady was in a coffin.

All of us had the overwhelming sense that the person at the church door had had some connection to this woman, and so strong was the sense of telepathy that we all had the feeling that there would be a message left on the church answerphone. It was one of those times when we all just knew what was coming next.

We walked to the part of the hall where the phone was and realized that Jim had at least unplugged it, but the answerphone had a red light on it that flashed when there was a message and it was indeed flashing furiously now.

When I pressed the playback button there was an anxious-sounding woman speaking, saying, 'Hello, I'm trying to get someone in the church to contact me. I need a Spiritualist minister to conduct my mother's funeral. Can someone please call me back on this number?'

Well, I did call her and she told me that she'd come to the door of the church but no one had been there, so she'd left a message on the phone.

All of us in the circle had had the same sense of knowing that this lady's mother had visited our circle that night, and though her daughter hadn't been able to speak to anyone, she had made herself known.

I asked the woman on the phone if she was a Spiritualist like her mother and had a belief in life after death, and she told me that she did, so I felt it was right to pass on to her what had happened in our circle that night.

To say that she was astounded would be an understatement. It was quite amazing, as her mother had been called Agnes Wallace and she'd already decided that she would bury her in the camel-hair coat and scarf that she'd loved to wear in life. All of the other things that came through in the circle were accepted and the overall feeling was a happy one.

Remembering this story from that circle all those years ago takes my mind back to the energy we used to sit in each week. It was an amazing group and our connection to the spirit world just got stronger the longer we went on. With such a connection, your belief in the spirit world turns to absolute knowledge and trust. I honestly can't think why people would want to stop their development at any point and feel that they had moved on from it.

The close bond we built in that circle still remains today and though we have all moved on to different things and travelled in different directions in our lives, there's still an amazing amount of telepathic connection between us. Each of us still sits regularly in circle, though not together any more, and we all still tell each other when we need healing thoughts to be sent out or if someone needs help of any kind. I suppose our circles have just expanded and because of the love and telepathy between us we can be as distant as we like and our little circle still keeps growing.

Communication in the circle

Over the years I've had some quite amazing messages come through from the other side when I've worked in a circle. In some cases one medium in the group has got something and others have been given evidence to corroborate it, which always gives information more validity.

It still surprises me how powerful messages can be when there is harmony among people in a circle. As an individual, I give messages to tens of thousands of people, but when I am in my circle with my friends, the power somehow seems to be amplified and the messages much clearer.

I know that not everyone has access to a good private circle, but if you do, you should really try to make the most of your opportunity to work as a group mind rather than just further your own development.

Working as a team over the years, my current circle has brought through many important messages for people who are in our group and equally as many for those who aren't but who have a connection to one of us.

I recall that on one occasion our circle sat together in quiet meditation with no expectations of what the session would bring. We simply sent out prayers and good intentions to those we knew who had problems or loss in their life. As we sat there quietly contemplating and waiting to sense our spirit friends around us, each of us without knowing began to sense the same thing in the atmosphere.

From my own perspective, I sensed the presence of a young man who was standing in the centre of our little circle. It felt as though he was trying to get my attention in a way that someone would if they were standing somewhere in your space to be noticed, but he said nothing. I remember thinking to myself, Who is this?, *but nothing came back to me. I asked my spirit guide, who I could feel was building beside me, if he could help me bring this young visitor into our circle and in that split second I felt peace descend over me.*

I let it go, adjusted my mind to the quiet of the room again and sent out healing thoughts to some of the people who'd asked me to do so for friends and family and so on until I eventually felt it was time to come out of my meditation. Even though I had been focusing on healing, I was aware that something else had happened in our circle and I felt it was to do with our visitor.

As we went round each sitter afterwards, we found that every one of us had received something that related to a young man who had died and had visited us from the spirit world.

My friend on my right started when she said that her meditation had been broken by a vision of a young man in his late teens lying on a bed. She felt that he had died in that room.

It went on with the next sitter. She'd also had a vision, but it had all been to do with taking drugs. She had seen needles and other drug-related items.

Our next sitter had heard the name 'Garry' and felt there had been a terrible accident involving a young man and drugs.

On it went and at the end of our discussion we were able to piece things together. One of the women in our circle had a neighbour whose son, Garry, had died in very mysterious circumstances that were still under investigation by the police. Four of our group had heard the word 'accident' and three of us felt that he wanted help somehow. We all knew that the help he required was to get this message to his family, as there was a question of suicide surrounding his death and it felt as though he wanted this to be cleared up with his family. Our circle member told us that rumours of suicide were certainly flying around the estate where she lived.

There was one little detail that one of our guys picked up that seemed insignificant at the time but turned out to be important. He reported that he'd seen the young man during his meditation and had also seen a mobile phone showing a text message that he couldn't make out.

My friend said that she'd speak to her neighbour if she got the right moment to do so and we left it at that.

It must have been a month later that she was able to pass on the information to the mother of the young man. Apparently she was happy to receive it. She told my friend that her son had been using drugs, but she was sure that he hadn't been suicidal. There had been an inquest into his death two weeks after our circle and it had backed this up. One of the things that had come to light was that he'd bought drugs from a person who was selling unrefined heroin on the street, which had resulted in two other young people in the area dying in the same manner and several near-deaths. The name of that dealer had been found on a text message on Garry's phone when it had been examined by the investigators.

I don't know what happened in the follow-up to this investigation, but I do know that the boy's mother took some comfort from the fact that her son hadn't ended his life by his own hand.

This is just one example of the results that can come from a circle. I believe that when we sit together as a team it helps to strengthen our connection and trust in the spirit world. I've often felt that much of my own individual success as a medium at that time was helped by those who sat with me for all those years.

Starting a circle

When I'm teaching courses to new students I always encourage them to start their own circles. In the old days people were told not to sit in a circle unless they had a fully trained medium with them, but I often think of the very first circles, which started with people who weren't knowledgeable about what they were doing. In some cases, all they had was blind trust. It was dedication and devotion that developed the mediums back then, so you don't have to be a medium to begin with, but you might end up being one as the circle develops.

Earlier I talked about preparing your mind for working with the spirit world. If you've understood all this and know that it's only your own fear that can disturb your mind then you'll understand that it's perfectly fine for anyone to start their own spiritual circle.

The way I started my private circle was simply for us to sit as a group and go through the meditation process and dedicate all the power we built to people we knew who needed it. This is the perfect way for any new group to start.

Things to look out for when you start a circle

✦   Try to resist looking for spiritual phenomena when you first begin a circle – chances are that you won't get any.

✦   Always remember that you are part of a group when you open up to spirit in this sacred space. Try to connect with the other sitters – no one should try to stand out in a good circle.

✦   Always try to be early or at least on time for your circle – remember, you've made an appointment with the spirit world. Try to keep it. In my own circle if a person was late then they didn't get in – in fact they wouldn't try to.

✦   If you find that for some reason you can't get into the power during a circle then just send out healing to others – doing something positive is better than struggling internally.

✦   Respect the person who runs your circle. If you find that you can't do this, you shouldn't be there.

✦   Some circles are staged in a dark or dimly lit room; this is only to create a sense of relaxation. I have sat in dark and light circles. It's all about choice.

✦   There are some circles that like to play meditation music in the background. Again it's about choice. Having sat in circles with and without music, I prefer not to have it, but that's my choice.

❖ Always keep a diary of your experiences for your own reference. You should also have someone record the experiences of each sitter for the circle's reference.

❖ It's also good to keep a healing list or book of the people who require help. If you leave the book out for the circle to see before you begin the practice, it makes it easier to remember them. Also, it reminds you of one of the reasons why you're doing this.

I honestly believe that when it comes to your circle, you should keep it simple and sincere and try to be patient with yourself as well as patient with others. Mrs Primrose's most famous words to me when I thought I was really taking my time were: 'In development you can never go slow enough.'

I understand this now and it is a must to be patient and try not to fill your mind with too many expectations all at once. Try to see the circle as a place where you can feel safe and open up your mind, but allow it to happen naturally. You'll come to know when you are forcing your development, or struggling in it, because nothing much will happen. Be patient. When it comes to the spirit world, what is for you will never go by you.

Universal circle online

There are many people out there who wish to develop spiritually but don't have access to a circle or people close to them who share the same type of spiritual interests. I do a lot of travelling with my work and I encounter many people who would love to be in a circle, but for one reason or another they simply can't. This gave me an idea.

One of my students from Germany lived in a small village with a very strong religious tone, where people frowned upon mediumship and even spiritual healing. She wanted to practise her healing and to build a small circle where she could develop spiritually and share her beliefs with like-minded others, but she was in a difficult situation. She was sure that if she advertised for people to start a spiritual group, some of the villagers would find out and some kind of a witch trial would follow. So she chose not to proceed.

One day during a seminar she told me about her plight and asked me what I thought she could do. After thinking about this, I offered her an idea that had flashed into my mind: I suggested that she sit on her own in her apartment at the same time as my circle.

I remember her looking at me strangely at first, but the more she thought about it, the more it began to make sense to her. Telepathy isn't restricted to a room, or even a country, so she could tune in and see if anything happened. What was there to lose?

She tried it and before long she was having the sense that she could see the people in my circle and even feel some of the things that we were picking up on. And in the same way, some of the circle could sometimes tune in to her.

We carried this on for several months until she moved to a place where she was invited into a very good private circle, and it showed me that she didn't need the physicality of the circle – it was the sense of belonging that gave her the telepathic link to the rest of the group and gave them the link to her.

So now I tell all my students to try to sit at seven o'clock on a Thursday evening; this is when my circle sits. Even if I'm not there, the rest of the group will sit. I especially want people who are on their own to sit at this time, as being linked to my circle will give a sense of purpose and connection to their meditation.

I started to invite people to do this about two years ago and now we have thousands of people doing it all over the world. Other circles are also connected to us. We find it to be a great way of connecting minds that wish to grow spiritually and of generating healing and compassion for others. I've been inundated with accounts of people who've felt the benefit of these healings. In fact my own brother is one of the many who have really been lifted by the power of our universal circle of healers.

Recently my oldest brother Tommy was given the sad news that he would have to lose his leg due to diabetes. Obviously the whole family was affected by the news and all of our hearts went out to him and his family. The first thing I did was to tell all my healers who sit each Thursday. We keep in touch through Facebook, which I think we might change to Faithbook in future! I believe it only took minutes and the word was out there and thousands of people said they would sit on the Thursday evening at seven o'clock UK time and send healing, either from their circles or individually.

It inspires me to think of all those thousands of people meditating at the same moment, no matter where they are or how far they are from one another. I'm certain that there is something even bigger we could do with this, but for my brother it was certainly enough. After his operation he was told that he would be in recovery for at least six months and that part of this would be to help him to cope with what had happened on an emotional level as well physically. One of the things that our family dreaded was that his spirits would sink, which would only be natural, but to our total surprise he seemed to go the opposite way.

Now my brother is in amazingly high spirits, and instead of taking six months to recover, he was walking with his prosthetic limb in just over six weeks. In fact not only walking – at my other brother Jonny's recent wedding, Tommy was one of the first to get up on the dance floor.

We have now collected hundreds of stories like Tommy's from our Facebook connection and it shows us that even if you are sitting on your own in development, you can be part of something bigger.

Sitting alone

If, for whatever reason, you are sitting alone, here are some pointers and an exercise to guide you:

❖ Try to sit in the same place each time, as I pointed out earlier, and make sure it's a place where you feel comfortable and balanced.

❖ Prepare the room as you wish, but remember it's all about turning your mind in a more spiritual direction.

❖ Start at the same time if you can, just as you would in a circle. It is respectful to the spirit world to show some dedication in where and when you sit.

Exercise: Sitting on your own

❖ Take your mind into the silence and breathe deeply and steadily.

❖ Relax your body and allow your breathing to find its own natural rhythm.

❖ Allow your mind to become peaceful. Just let any thoughts that come to you move through your mind. Don't become attached to anything.

❖ Sit still and focus your awareness on the emptiness in the space around you.

❖ Try to be aware of your own subtle energy in that atmosphere and to feel how expanded you can become at this auric level.

❖ Send a thought out to your spirit guide and welcome them into your space.

❖ Feel the presence of your spirit guide as you connect. Feel the calling card or signature that allows you to know your guide.

❖ Be aware that you are not only connected to your own guide but that you have the capacity to link with all the other circles who are sitting at the same time as you. Allow your subtle light body to feel connected at a higher level and just sit in the experience.

❖ Send out healing to this interconnected network of spiritual healing and just observe anything that comes to your mind.

❖ When you feel the experience is lessening, thank your guide and allow them to disconnect from your space.

❖ Start to breathe deeply into your chest until you feel ready to open your eyes and connect back to the room.

❖ Write down everything that you felt happened to you on the physical, auric and spiritual levels. Note anything you saw, felt or heard.

I have had reports from those who sit on their own but link into our circle at seven o'clock saying they feel the power that they sit in get much stronger during the meditation. I believe that connecting with others is so important in this regard. Even if only two people are sitting in the power together, they feel it much more strongly, and it is the strength of that power that boosts the signal out to the spirit world in the atmosphere around us.

Your magical time

Your circle is your magical time where you can experience the beauty and joy of your spirit guides and guardians, not to mention your loved ones on the other side, as they too can get closer to you in this sacred space. If you find that you have the opportunity to sit in a spiritual development circle, don't pass it by – it might be the beginning of an incredible part of your life.

For me the spiritual circle is my spiritual home, a place where many amazing people have visited me from this world and the next. It's a great chance to connect with the spirit world in a much clearer way and it also reminds us that we are part of a source that is infinite. In our small circles we create a little window where the light of that source can shine through. I truly believe that my mediumship and spirituality have remained strong over the years because I am regularly connected to that source through my weekly practice of sitting in my circle.

Being part of a circle also keeps us grounded when we get too 'out there', because our fellow sitters will notice very quickly if we start to become too flighty and need a reality check.

Reality check

A very important thing to note at the beginning of your development is that you allow yourself to have reality checks. By this, I mean that you should check in with yourself and make sure that you aren't allowing your mind to become too spaced out by all the spiritual processes you've become involved in.

I understand how easy it is for people to get disconnected from their everyday life when they begin to develop. Over the course of my own development I've witnessed people transforming in both good and bad ways.

Some years ago I was working with a Scandinavian group when I met a lovely young woman who I must say had the potential to be a great medium. She was in her mid-thirties and married with two children. Her husband was a professional man and though not totally a believer in life after death, he did support his wife's claims that she was a medium and that she used her work to help people.

Almost a year later I ran into her again at a spiritual congress in southern Germany and I remember that it took me a moment or two to register who she was. Her bright blue eyes told me she was the same Scandinavian woman, but instead of her usual attire, she was in long, flowing, baggy robes, and in place of the short, neatly cut brown hair, she had bleached blonde hair hanging wildly around her shoulders.

It was a strange moment because I felt that she was so different, not only because of the hair but because of her whole demeanour. I was certain when we shared a hug that she was aware of my uneasy feeling, as I sensed that she shared it.

I went about my business that day and tried to put the feeling out of my mind, as well as any thoughts about this woman. We were both at a spiritual congress and there were many people there who were dressed like her. I also knew as a hairdresser that women tended to change their hair colour as a protest or to rebel in some way, and I'd always thought of this woman as feisty and in control of her life, so that shouldn't have bothered me. I do remember thinking, though, that there was something inside her that had changed and I rather hoped I would run into her again and maybe even have a chat and try to sense what was happening with her.

It was late the following day before we met again. I saw her across the room, in good spirits and surrounded by people dressed similarly to her. She made her way through some of them to come over to me and tell me that she was completely ecstatic, as she was leaving with a group to go into a totally new dimension.

'You should join us,' she said. 'You would love it.'

But something in me said I wouldn't.

I knew in my heart of hearts that this very balanced woman had walked away from her ordinary life and was now on a spiritual journey with no boundaries. My heart began to sink and I tried to ask her about her old life and her husband and children, but she kept talking over me, telling me that before she'd been living in a world full of non-realities and that today she wanted just to be in the now with her new reality – the only reality that was important.

She confided in me that she was awaiting the arrival of a spiritual master, a teacher who would be arriving soon from another world. It was located on the other side of the universe, but he was making the journey and would be here very soon to teach her group.

After some more garbled talk like this, I decided I'd had enough. I knew that this woman had lost touch with her rational mind.

I never saw her again after that and I don't recall any intergalactic guru touching down on Earth in the past 10 years or so either. I did, however, find out through a mutual friend that this poor lady had suffered a breakdown and been institutionalized for quite some time before, thankfully, landing back with her very compassionate husband and family.

One can only hope that when the mind becomes fixated on the ridiculous like this, the loss of rationality isn't permanent. It can happen to people who easily become ungrounded, which I never felt that woman would be, but fantasy can be powerful.

In a case similar to this, I recall a very intelligent man who got involved in a strange cult. He was caught soon afterwards creating crop circles and claiming that they were a sign from his high master that he was coming to offer the President of the United States the chance to change the world.

Fantasy and imagination always have to be kept under control when you walk the spiritual path, as you're already dealing with a subject that is difficult to prove in a world of logic.

In every circle I've been part of we've had reality checks where we've sat as a group and had open discussions about where we are with our spiritual development and our experiences and beliefs. Mrs Primrose always told us that the material world was the one that was most important to us and that we should always remain connected to our physical life and all the important things in it, like family, friends and jobs.

Many people give all these up to go off and find themselves spiritually. This is a personal choice and if you are a responsible adult and you make such a decision then you have to live with the results. When these affect the people in your life and bring them heartbreak, you have some responsibility to face up to as well. Remember, the spirit world doesn't ask us to make these big decisions – they are *our* decisions.

Everyone I know on the spiritual path has come through many difficult times, as have most people in this world. That is just part of the human condition. I've seen people who've believed that a spiritual force has ended something good in their life, and as far as I'm aware that hasn't really been the case, but it is much easier for some people to blame an invisible force than to take ownership of the difficult stuff in their life.

One woman I know said that Elvis Presley was sending her messages, and one of those messages was that she should leave her husband and move in with a workmate. Now I don't know about you, but I've no idea why Elvis would have any interest in who lives with whom, or indeed who should leave whom. Always check the messages that come through your mediumship and try to prove anything you can – never take things for granted.

As well as the people who go off the rails from time to time on their journey, there are, however, many cases where people change in a very positive and constructive way because of their spiritual development, and I'm happy to say that I know many of them.

My own young student Steven, who came to me very confused and who used to worry about everyone and expect the worst, is now not only a medium and an extremely good healer, but a person whose attitude towards life has become much stronger because of his regular meditation and spiritual work.

The great thing about Steven was that he realized that this was a process that would take time and that no amount of rushing would change that. This, I feel, is the true key to success in spiritual development. Don't be in a rush to get there. It's a cliché, but it really is all about the journey. 'Anything worth doing is worth doing well,' is another one, and there is truth in that too.

I would hope that wherever you are in your development you do your best to honour your spiritual gifts, respect your spirit guides and be true to yourself. Mediumship can be a magnificent experience, but remember humility as often as you can.

Chapter 7

SHARING YOUR GIFT

You'll know when it's time to start to share your gift with others, because by this point you'll have had many experiences where the spirit world has given you information that you've checked out and found to be true.

On one occasion during my meditation my guide showed me a scene in which he was taking part in a ceremony in China back in the fifth century. There were many details in this episode that I could follow up on. None of the knowledge given was anything I'd ever heard of before. I had no idea of the names, dates, places or even the costumes of that particular period in that particular country. It was only after many months of research in the public library that I discovered that each component of the vision was relevant to the life that my guide had lived. This told me I was being given evidence by an intelligent force from the other side.

There were also many incidents in my own development circle where spirits gave me information for other sitters that I couldn't have known prior to the session. The details not only turned out to be true but also relevant for them at the time. In a circle it's easier to verify information, as you have a collection of people you can work with, but even if you're sitting on your own you can still test the source of your information by asking for details that you can check out through historical records.

Before working with the public you should have many experiences of the spirit world passing correct information to you that you couldn't have gained in any other way. Each success will help build your confidence in your mediumship and eventually you'll know you're ready to start working with the public. If, however, you find you get information in your mind that never turns out to have any relevance, don't rush the process. It's okay to go back to sitting in the power for a while.

When you do reach the point of sharing your gift with the public, you can make a difference to many people's lives, and that's the best motivation for what you're doing – that and good intentions.

Marcus was an example of how a life can be changed by a message from spirit. He was a man in his early forties who had lost his wife, Gabriella, in a terrible car crash right in front of his home in a beautiful suburban part of Switzerland.

I first met him 10 months afterwards, when he was still very raw and exhausted by his emotions. Our meeting had been set up by a mutual friend who had attended some of my seminars over the years. When he'd told me of Marcus's situation, I'd felt compelled to see the man at once.

We met in a hotel I was staying at in Basel. On first meeting this poor man I didn't have to be a medium to tell that he was in the deep realms of grief. This is something all mediums will encounter as they work on the spiritual path. A big part of our training is learning to separate our own emotions from those of the sitter, as it will do no good to become immersed in someone else's emotional turmoil. In the early days of your practice, you might find this difficult because of how overwhelming it feels, but preparing your mind with the idea that this is not your pain or suffering and that you may have a great opportunity to help and heal can help you separate from the sitter's situation and focus on trying to lift them out of it.

Even though I knew the circumstances of Gabriella's death, I still had to find evidence of her spirit life and hopefully a message that might help her husband to move back into his own life again.

As I began to tune in to Marcus I became aware of Gabriella's presence and heard her say her name to me. It felt as though she was speaking inside my head rather than in my ear. I could sense that she was really making a strong connection with me as I just began to speak spontaneously and heard myself making statement after statement to her husband sitting opposite me.

This type of mediumship is the strongest I know. It almost feels as though my mind has been overshadowed by the communicating spirit. It's not something that I can teach to others, as it honestly only happens when I've truly bonded with a spirit, as I knew I had with Gabriella. From past experience I was aware that I shouldn't question it, just go with the flow until it stopped.

I believe that I spoke like this for 30-odd minutes before I looked for a response from Marcus. He was staring at me with a look of surprise on his face and his head was shaking slightly from side to side. I noticed for the first time that he was holding a notepad in his hand. He looked at it for a moment, then he told me that he'd come prepared with 40 questions that he would ask his wife if he made contact with her and that in my long diatribe I'd answered 39 of them without prompting.

It was Marcus's first experience of sitting with a medium and he hadn't known what to expect. He'd had his doubts, but he'd been hoping so much *that his wife would know his questions because he'd asked them all out loud to her in his empty bedroom at home. If she did know them, it would be more proof for him.*

He never did ask me the last question, as he said he felt it was too personal, and as his wife had answered all the others but not this one, he thought that she felt it was too personal as well.

He was stunned by what had happened and I spent an hour or so with him just chatting and explaining a little more about life after death and the spirit world, as I felt that as well as the questions he'd brought he might want to enquire about other things that had occurred during the reading.

At the close of our session I couldn't help but notice that Marcus looked much lighter than when we'd first met, and he even sounded stronger when he spoke to me before leaving the hotel room. It was one of those readings that I always hope will happen – a reading where someone who is truly in the thick of grief at least gets their mind working and questioning again. As mediums, we might not always be able to help, but we should always try our best.

Three years later I was in southern Germany and I was asked if I would see Marcus again, as he was working in the same area. I was curious to find out how he was getting on with his life and I was certain in my gut that there would be a positive change around him.

Once again we met in a hotel room and once again his wife came through immediately and fired a barrage of spontaneous answers at him, which I noticed made him smile. It dawned on me that I hadn't seen him smile before and how different he looked when his face lit up.

There seemed to be a real feeling of excitement going on in his life and he was involved in all sorts of new ventures, so much so that I felt a buzz around me when Gabriella communicated.

Just six months before our meeting Marcus had been introduced to a lady of his own age through some mutual friends. She had been widowed around much the same time as his wife had passed and in a very short time the couple had begun to bond. I suppose that it was understandable, as they could really connect through their sense of loss.

Now Gabriella was coming to give her blessing to her husband moving on with his life. Since the last reading he'd been so aware that she was still connected to him, and he was hoping she'd know he'd met someone who was interested in him and would give her approval, which of course she did.

For me, it was just so good to listen to this man who'd looked as though he would never progress in his life after such a tragedy. To see him looking forward again made me feel very uplifted and happy for him.

It was a very personal reading again and I don't believe it's necessary to share all the details of Marcus's life, but I did learn that the last question from the previous reading had been about him joining his wife on the spirit side of life and the fact that she'd refused to answer it had told him that she didn't want that.

I also believe that Gabriella was in some way responsible for guiding her husband to his new lady and that she is very happy for him and for her.

I often tell people that there really is life after death, and I mean that for those living in this world too. When someone we love dies, there is still a part of their consciousness living in the spirit world and it is that higher, more spiritual part that wants to see us move on and keep living, and not in pain. Our loved ones in spirit always want us to be happy in this life, no matter what.

Distant readings

Something that more and more mediums are doing today is distant readings via Skype, Facetime and so on.

However, since such things have come into our everyday life, I've only ever done this kind of distant reading on two occasions.

The first was for a woman who was in California and was so desperate to have a reading that she suggested Skype. As it was totally new to me, I had a friend help me to set it up. During this reading the sitter, who I could see on the screen, often became tearful and I felt that I was unable to comfort her properly. Also, because there were often delays in communication, the whole thing felt quite disjointed. Even so, at the end of our session the lady appeared to have the answers she was seeking. From my point of view, though, I never felt a part of the experience, as I would have if I'd been in the same room.

From this first experience I learned that mediumship can be done like this. Fair enough – why wouldn't it? Remember, there are people who get information from the spirit world to pass on to their loved ones when they aren't even present, so that isn't a problem. Also, for many years mediums have sometimes had to give a reading over the phone when they couldn't be with a sitter. That is something I've only done a handful of times over 30 years. I always feel that the communication works much better when you're sitting in the person's actual energy, and that if you're physically present you can be a comfort to them if they need you to be. Also, they sometimes feel the strength of the spirit in the room and that can be just as evidential to them as the messages themselves.

So I felt that distant mediumship wasn't anything I wanted to repeat. However, recently I was asked to give an online reading to a couple in Australia and I realized that their situation was such that online communication was the only way to help them.

As we started, I tried to tune in as I would have done if they'd been sitting facing me and in a short time I was feeling the presence of their young daughter, who had died as a result of an accident. I found that it helped me to keep the link if they didn't say much to me, as the delays in their answers seemed to break my contact with their daughter, so I asked them simply to say 'yes' or 'no' unless I got something through that I wasn't sure about.

Many different details started to come to me and I found that most of them were forming like pictures in my mind in a clairvoyant way. Each time I saw something I would reveal what I was seeing and wait a moment to have it confirmed before moving on to the next picture. Like all mediumship, it worked better when I could create a kind of flow.

Madeleine was their daughter's name. I saw it written like a banner when I closed my eyes. Then I got a description of what she looked like and what she'd been wearing the last time her parents saw her alive.

The more I got into the reading, the stronger the information became, but all the time I had the feeling that I wanted to be closer to the parents physically. It seemed to me that no matter how accurate the information was or how significant, there was still something missing from my perspective.

Madeleine gave me enough information to satisfy her parents that she was coming through and then she moved on to the message she wanted to convey to them. I was now hearing her – the pictures that had begun the reading were now coming to me as dialogue in my head. I also became aware that I was speaking quite spontaneously with the parents and just allowing the information to flow as best I could. Madeleine told them that she wished they'd talk to each other and that she didn't want their marriage to fall apart because of her death.

I knew that this information was important to the couple, because they were both nodding at me and saying they understood, and then they hugged and held each other.

The message their daughter gave them was one that I've passed to many parents in this situation and what gave it more credibility was that she gave me the exact sentences they'd said to each other during arguments. She didn't want them to carry on speaking like this. She knew that they were both hurting and she didn't want them to inflict their pain on each other.

Then there was a moment when I just lost the connection and my mediumship stopped. It felt to me that the message had been given and that was all that was going to happen. There was a sense that Madeleine's information had to be presented like that so her parents would be left with her exact sentiment and that I wasn't to add anything else to it. That was why she left almost abruptly.

At the end of such a reading I always ask people if they have any questions they'd like to ask me about what they've just experienced, and even in this situation I thought it was right to do so, though the online connection was breaking up and it was now difficult to communicate clearly. The father was saying something to me, but I couldn't make it out.

Then the link was lost altogether and I had to do the end of the session by telephone. I answered the couple's questions about the afterlife, but it did concern me that the disconnection might have happened at a very critical moment during the reading.

The upshot of this is that I really would rather see people face to face when it comes to personal readings. It somehow feels much more authentic to me. I know that spirit communication can work through any means, but I believe in being the best I can be, and my limited experience of online reading has convinced me that it isn't for me. I'm certain that the new generation of mediums will take to internet readings much more readily and proficiently than I have. There is no space or time in the spirit world and I believe that when spirits are truly with us anything is possible, so I watch all of the new ways to communicate in our world with deep interest. But all I can say is that to do the best I can for people and the spirit world, I must do what feels right for me, and nothing beats the personal touch.

'Why do I do this?'

I could tell you hundreds of stories about the wonderful experiences I've had in my life as a medium, but one comes to mind that I believe was given to me when I needed to be reminded of why I've dedicated my life to this practice.

When I was working in my barber's shop in Glasgow some years ago, often when my day's work was done I would head off to a Spiritualist church and give a demonstration of mediumship. So I'd find that I wouldn't arrive back home until very late some nights, and after several years of this, one day I started to wonder why I was doing it.

That day stands out in my mind because I wanted to go to a concert in Glasgow with my friends that night. Tina Turner was playing at one of the football stadiums and we all had tickets, only I'd suddenly remembered that I was booked to work in a Spiritualist church in Edinburgh. My heart sank. I loved my mediumship, but the sinking feeling made me wonder why I couldn't cancel that booking and go to the concert instead. Then, as my mind sank further, I questioned my motives for doing mediumship at all.

It was one of those days we all get from time to time, and I am no different from anyone else. I recall that I didn't spend much time engaging with my clients during haircuts as my mind was filled with Why do I do mediumship? Why?

The day came to a close and all the staff left. I was beginning to clean the salon when someone popped their head under the half-shut door. It was a man I'd never seen before. He was somewhere in his early forties, I thought. I wasn't in the best frame of mind, so when he asked me if he could have a shave I was surprised when the words 'Of course you can' came out of my mouth. Part of me wanted to tell him no, but I honestly had so much time on my hands before heading to Edinburgh that I just got on with it.

I escorted him to where we did shaves and he lay back in the large leather chair.

As I began to put shaving soap over his face and neck, I remember once again thinking to myself, Why me?

Then, when I looked up at my face in the mirror, I was rooted to where I stood. A woman was looking right back at me.

I did a double-take. I knew she wasn't standing in the salon, but I had to check to make sure. She wasn't there. But when I turned back, she was still in the mirror. She was my height and slim, with short blonde hair that she was tucking neatly behind her ears. She was wearing a short black dress that made her look quite chic, I thought.

The man was tilted back with his eyes closed, so I knew he couldn't see the woman. By now I was feeling the presence of spirit around me the way I always did when I was about to get a message for someone. Oh no, *I thought,* how can I tell a strange man that there's a spirit woman here who wants to give him a message from the other side? He only came in for a shave.

Of course the man had no idea that I was a medium, and I had no idea what his reaction would be if I shared this with him, but the more I looked at the lady, the stronger the feeling became that I had to speak to him.

Then I heard her voice inside my head, saying, 'Tell him I am here. My name is Judy.'

Somehow I plucked up the courage to explain to the man that I was a medium and to give him a description of Judy. He sat bolt upright in a flash and looked straight into my eyes, but from the corner of my right eye I was looking over at Judy, who was opening her hand while inwardly I was thinking to her, Why are you here? What is your message?

'Thanks for the lollipops.'

That was what came back and I saw that there were three little lollipops in the palm of her hand.

Somehow I forced the words out of my mouth to the man staring wildly back at me.

With that Judy was gone and I was left looking at a man who was sobbing and then really crying heavily into his chest.

Soon he recovered enough to tell me that Judy was his wife who had died six months earlier and the description I'd given him fitted her perfectly: she always wore this type of outfit and it was characteristic of her to do the thing with her hair. But it was the lollipops I wanted to know about.

What had happened was that three days earlier his seven-year-old son had asked if he could take lollipops to his mother's grave instead of flowers. The man told me that when he'd heard his wife thank him for them, it filled his heart with hope because it meant that she could still see him and his son and he realized that somehow, somewhere, she would always be able to watch over him.

That very day I'd been asking myself why I did this work and I felt that the spirit world had answered both of us with this message.

I really don't doubt my work any more, or even ask why I do it, because seeing people like this man lifted up and given hope and encouragement to go on with their lives is reason enough for me. Every medium will get their own proof that will help them stay on the path when they have moments of doubt, and I truly hope that if you are ever lost or doubtful you will let my journey inspire you.

I wish all of you the greatest success with your mediumship because this means that many more people will get help and just as many will get the message that I share wherever I go with my work: 'You can't die. You can't die for the life of you.'

Conclusion

The mediumship journey isn't always easy, but if you find it part of your nature, you will battle through, no matter what. I hope you all take into account that it is the highs and lows that make this journey special and that without the trials and tribulations, the tests and hurdles before you, it would have less meaning or purpose.

Many people have a spiritual gift and choose not to use it for one reason or another, but those of you who feel compelled to step onto my path and develop your craft with a view to helping others have begun an amazing adventure in your life.

Remember, as you grow spiritually and sensitively, you'll become more aware of your own spirit and so many new things will open up to you. Though this book is a course for beginners, it provides a foundation that will stay with you no matter how far you progress. These basic step-by-step teachings always offer a point to go back to if you become confused or stuck.

Always try to take the time to process what you have learned and never be afraid to take stock of how your spiritual development is affecting your everyday life and the people in it. All spiritual development should enhance your life and help you to gain a better understanding of this life and what it is truly about, but it won't happen overnight. With this in mind, always be prepared to be patient, because you'll soon learn that just when you think you've accomplished something special, there's a whole lot more still to be learned.

Spiritual development is a lifelong journey, and the sooner you learn this, the easier it will become for you, but please try to relax and enjoy the process.

ABOUT THE AUTHOR

Angela Nott

Gordon Smith is hailed as 'the UK's best medium', renowned for his astonishing ability to pinpoint exact names of people, places and even streets relevant to a person's life.

From early childhood, Gordon had the ability to see, sense and hear spirit people. At the age of 24, he embarked on 15 years of study and practice, going on to develop his abilities as a medium – or messenger from the spirit world – under the tutelage of some of the great legends of the spiritualist church.

Gordon is now a bestselling author and one of the world's top psychic mediums and spiritual teachers, conducting mediumship workshops and events around the world. His Celtic charm and lively demonstrations – delivered in his trademark style combining humour, pure passion and empathy towards others – provide his audiences with a rare opportunity to experience the fascinating phenomenon of mediumship.

www.gordonsmithmedium.com

Notes

Notes

Notes

HAY HOUSE

Look within

Join the conversation about latest products, events, exclusive offers and more.

f Hay House UK

🐦 @HayHouseUK

📷 @hayhouseuk

❤ healyourlife.com

We'd love to hear from you!

Notes